IMPROVE YOUR
WINDSURFING

IMPROVE YOUR WINDSURFING

PETER HART

Willow Books
Collins
8 Grafton Street, London W1
1988

Willow Books
William Collins Sons & Co Ltd
London · Glasgow · Sydney · Auckland
Toronto · Johannesburg

First published 1988
© Sackville Design Group Ltd

BRITISH LIBRARY CATALOGUING IN PUBLICATION DATA
Hart, Peter
Improve your windsurfing.——(Improve your sport).
1. Windsurfing
I. Title   II. Series
797.3′3   GV811.63.W56

ISBN 0-00-218301-3

Designed by Sackville Design Group Ltd
78 Margaret Street, London W1N 7HB
Art director: Al Rockall
Art editor: Joyce Chester
Editor: Lorraine Jerram
Illustrations: David Cringle
Set in Melior by Bookworm Typesetting, Manchester
Printed and bound in Italy by New Interlitho S.P.A. Milan

The author: Peter Hart, top
competitive windsurfer
and dedicated enthusiast. He is
highly regarded as an
exponent of windsurfing technique

Taking a look at windsurfing's brief history is both interesting and informative. Blessed with hindsight, we may chuckle at the ungainly antics of early windsurfing man as we picture him wrestling with crude equipment. A closer study, however, reveals a direct relationship between design and technique. By noting the problems encountered by the pioneers on those early boards and the steps they took to alleviate them, we can begin to understand the source of inspiration for all those humps, bumps, curves and hollows that adorn the modern funboard. In the more recent past, manufacturers pandered to the whims of a desperately trend-conscious market and built boards and sails that were unsuitable both for the average weather conditions and the general standard of the windsurfing public. It is important to be able to distinguish between the fashionable and the functional, and to understand to what extent your own progress can be halted or accelerated by equipment ancient and modern.

It's all history

The question of who invented windsurfing (boardsailing, sailboarding, funboarding etc.) has become a topic of more interest to the legal buff than to the windsurfer, involving one of the longest-running patent disputes in the history of law. It is something of a shame that the imagination of the pioneers has been overshadowed by a saga of writs and royalties.

There is no doubt, however, that while such men as Newman Darby, Rainer Schwarz and Peter Chilvers all constructed primitive craft that used the free sailing principle (steering using the rig), it was Hoyle Schweitzer and, in the beginning, his partner Jim Drake who were responsible for developing and marketing the sport of windsurfing as we know it today.

Once upon a Windsurfer

In 1968 Schweitzer and Drake created the original Windsurfer, the board which lent the sport is generic name. It is a remarkable achievement that their original design, despite huge advancements in board and rig technology since then, is still in the marketplace today, albeit in modified form. On the racing front, the Windsurfer One Design Class remains active in many countries, Australia and the USA for example, and remains a favourite with freestyle specialists.

Windsurfing's forerunners, who include such relentless performers as Mike Walze, Matt Schweitzer (son of inventor Hoyle), Alex Aguera and Ken Winner, were getting restless. They felt this new sport had more to offer than just sailing up and down on flat water doing a few tricks. So, spurred on by a fiercely competitive spirit born out of their surfing and sailing backgrounds, they felt compelled to take their stock Windsurfers out into the mountainous Pacific surf on their doorsteps in Hawaii and California.

Thanks to modern boards and rigs, the thrills of strong-wind sailing and even funboard racing can be enjoyed by most keen windsurfers

American Alex Aguera, still a world-class competitor today, practises his freestyle routine on the original Windsurfer in 1976

The late Angus Chater, an Englishman who made his home beside the Hawaiian surf, flies one of the first fat-tailed 'jump' boards

Here was the sport in its purest form – surfing with the wind.

Sheer bravado and athleticism gave them some success as they hurtled down the faces of mountainous rollers, but long swims, battered bodies and broken rigs soon convinced them that, while the original design was fine for moderate winds and flat water sailing, it was hopelessly inadequate to cope with the rigours of high-wind surf sailing. They had two choices: either change the design or keep swimming.

The changes

1 The daggerboard, essential for stability and upwind performance in light winds, was a positive nuisance once the wind reached the force 4 mark. Above a certain speed, it would start to hydroplane, rise to the surface and capsize the board without warning. The problem was alleviated by the introduction of a smaller, swept-back 'storm dagger'.

2 Footstraps Initial forays through the surf were as safe as a game of Russian roulette. If the intrepid sailor was not washed from his board by the white water, then, as he took off from the top of the first wave, board and pilot would inevitably part company with a spectacular, sometimes messy and often expensive conclusion. One of the first men to attach footstraps to his Windsurfer was Larry Stanley; it is an invention that now bubbles out of almost every board on the market.

3 Twin fins At high speed in waves, directional stability is all-important and a feature which the original board with its single, floppy central fin did not possess in large quantities. The obvious cure was to insert a second fin parallel to the first.

4 Too big, too slow Ultimately, there was too much board in the water, which caused excess drag and made it painfully slow to manoeuvre in tight situations. The first adjustments were seen on the Windsurfer Rocket (the first production 'jump board'), where on the same hull both the mastfoot and the daggerboard were moved further aft. This had the effect of reducing the wetted area and allowed the board to plane on its tail at higher speeds. However, the board was still

It's all history

big and landed from the smallest jumps with a knee-wrenching thud. The next and most daring step to date was to saw off a section of the tail. The resulting short board was nicknamed the 'chopper' and, although still big, heavy and cumbersome next to today's wave boards, it pointed the way ahead.

5 Sails at that stage were primitive and for many years were to develop at a slower rate than boards. Nevertheless, to prevent the end of the sail dragging in the waves, the clew was cut higher and hollow-leeched storm and all-weather sails were made for high winds. It was not until the early 1980s that stabilized sail materials and full-length battens began to revolutionize sail design.

Meanwhile in Europe...
Thanks to the aforementioned hardy band of trail-blazers, Hawaii was to remain the centre of windsurfing innovation. However, the strength of the patent in the USA had stifled the healthy industrial rivalry that stimulates growth and, commercially, the country became stagnant. It was, ironically, in chilly Europe that the sport was to explode.

Unable to supply a growing market, Schweitzer granted the Dutch firm Ten Cate a licence to manufacture the original Windsurfer. Other licences were granted to firms such as Fred Ostermann's Windglider, Hi Fly, Sailboard and later Mistral.

No one could have predicted the speed with which windsurfing was to sweep across Europe in the early 1980s; here was a sport that somehow embodied all the fresh, healthy,

youthful exuberance of surfing yet you did not need to live in a Volkswagen camper van to be a part of it. For those landlocked in central Europe, it also represented the perfect summer alternative to snow skiing.

Sadly, such rampant growth was not to be healthy. Hundreds of rogue manufacturers emerged, many choosing simply to ignore the licence agreement and the 7.5 per cent per board royalty fee, others setting up in countries like France where Schweitzer, being short of money at the time, failed to register his patent.

'Pile it high, sell it cheap' was the adage, as rivers of throw-away boards flowed in and out of hypermarkets, service stations and, of course, the hundreds of new windsurfing shops. Within a couple of years, everyone had bought a slice of the new craze in the bargain basement. But their faces were soon to drop as they watched their new toys crack and break up almost as quickly as the companies who had made them.

Many fell by the wayside. People were still windsurfing in huge numbers but there were far too many companies trying to supply a dwindling growth end. Fortunately, the best survived but, for some years to come, were guilty of pandering to fashion and supplying the windsurfing public with what they thought they wanted and not what they needed.

Race vs jumps
At this stage, around 1981–82, there came a definite parting of the ways in the windsurfing world. On the one hand, windsurfing was coming more under the wing of dinghy sailing. The

manufacturers were quick to see the promotional possibilities in standard Olympic-style triangle racing, especially the open class. Well-branded prototypes at the front of the fleet were a sure way to boost sales. On the other, it was drifting back to its surfing roots as news of the wave jumping phenomenon wafted in from exotic shores.

Both trends were to bring about exciting new designs, although the benefits were not immediately apparent. The racing machines grew and grew. Enormous displacement hulls proved to be the answer to dynamic light-wind performance but had little relevance in the marketplace since they were hollow and therefore hopelessly fragile, as well as horribly unstable downwind and not much fun to sail off the race course. Recreational boards remained heavy but at least the manufacturers' involvement in racing forced them to research ways to make boards both strong and light.

However, while not everyone wanted to race, it seemed that they were all drunk on Hawaiian hype and wanted 'jump boards', even though they only sailed on sheltered lakes that entertained a gusty force 3 perhaps twice a year. Not only was central Europe seriously devoid of high winds and waves, but also very few had the skill at that time to sail this type of board.

The boards themselves were developments of the Rocket and 'chopper'. To promote jumps (carved turns had yet to be made public), they were short with thick, wide tails and were typified by such immortal designs as the Surf Line 'Egg', the Icarus and the

The 'ins and outs' at the 1981 Pan Am Cup. The boards were still long and heavy, but this style of strong wind, big wave, action-packed competition pointed the way ahead

Pure Juice 'Wave Hopper'. It was pitiful to see so many people struggling with these short, tippy boards in light winds, up to their ankles in water, when what they really needed was something with enough volume to support comfortably their weight.

The funboard revolution

The all-round funboard was the brainchild of German Peter Brockhaus, founder of the F2 Board Company (Fun and Function) and very much the father of European windsurfing. He sought to lead people away from impractical, specialized 'jump' boards and the idea that you needed huge winds and waves to be a real windsurfer. He spread the healthy news that high-performance sailing could take place with a wind speed as low as eleven knots on flat water. The tool he proposed was a design that possessed all the essential Hawaiianesque trimmings, was stable at high speeds, could footsteer and even jump, but which, most importantly, incorporated that all-important ingredient of volume to give it a passable light-wind performance.

'Das funboard!' was an unfortunate term in that it implied that windsurfing was only 'fun' if you were screaming along at twenty knots. The label stuck, however, and is used today to describe boards of all sizes, from sinker to course racer, designed with planing conditions in mind. Since it is virtually impossible nowadays to buy a board without footstraps, it is surprising that the whole sport is not called 'funboarding'. Gratefully, this is not the case.

Pan Am fever

Perhaps the single greatest influence on design and technique in the 1980s was the legendary Pan Am Cup. There were many who quite rightly felt that dinghy-style racing displayed the fast, visually exciting windsurfers in a very dull light. The Pan Am Cup, the first ever professional regatta, represented a radical departure. Racing was to take place in a minimum wind strength of force 4; it was to include several disciplines including 'ins and outs' (a figure-of-eight course in and out of the surf), a marathon, and, of course, wave performance. Where possible, the courses were laid inshore in full view of the spectators.

The first Cup in 1980 took place in winds that rarely dropped below force 6 and fired the imaginations of the windsurfing public. Although future events were almost becalmed, no one was in any doubt that this style of high-wind racing was the direction windsurfing should take.

With Peter Brockhaus again at the fore, the top pros competed around an international circuit for the Eurofun Cup, which subsequently became today's World Cup. Manufacturers submitted teams and used the regattas as testing grounds for new products. Concentrated research and development (trial and error) and feedback from the World Cup's three disciplines – racing, slalom and wave performance – have brought about tremendous changes in production equipment.

It is a healthy situation. The modern long funboard has all the racing benefits of speed and manoeuvrability but is still very easy to use. Weighing up to 10kg less than its counterpart of a decade ago, it has obliterated the legendary 'force 4 barrier'. It took immense strength, fitness and a lot of fancy footwork just to remain upstanding on the original plank in a breeze, but today most people with time to practise can be handling such winds comfortably within a couple of months. They can then display skills that would have turned heads on a Hawaiian beach a few years ago.

The sport today

To many, windsurfing is simply a way people find to make a fool of themselves on holiday, falling relentlessly off slippery planks under the not-so-watchful eye of a Greek/Spanish/French gigolo. Windsurfing today, however, supports a huge board, sail, accessories, holiday and fashion industry worth millions. In the UK alone there are over 200 registered schools, 1800 qualified instructors and at least 160,000 active participants with the world figure well into the millions. The sport is practised in every developed country in the world from Russia to Scandinavia, from Hawaii to New Zealand, and is growing at an estimated fifteen per cent every year.

Apart from encouraging mass participation, the sport has reached the following dizzy heights:

Olympic sport
In the 1984 Los Angeles Games, a fleet of Windgliders competed around the same course and to the same rules as the other yachting classes, thereby making windsurfing the youngest sport ever to be granted Olympic status. The first windsurfing gold medal winner was Dutchman Stefan van den Berg, who has since become one of the most successful professionals on the World Cup circuit.

Professional sport
The World Cup Series is windsurfing's showpiece. The winner is lauded as the best all-round sailor in the world, a title which, since the Cup's inception, has belonged exclusively to the indomitable American Robby Naish. The circus plays in

La Torche, France. Big sponsorship and huge crowds create a Grand Prix atmosphere at World Cup events

Japan, France, the USA, Germany and Holland, and regularly attracts crowds of 100,000 spectators who pack the beaches of La Torche in Brittany and Scheveningen on the Dutch coast to see their heroes in action.

Fastest sailing craft
In the summer of 1986 on the south end of the island of Fuertaventura in the Canaries, a windsurfer became the world's fastest sail-powered craft. Frenchman Pascal Maka reached the

The fastest sailor in the world – Pascal Maka blasts down the famous speed course at Weymouth, England

*The greatest adventurer of them all, the illustrious
Baron Arnaud de Rosnay. When the ocean claimed
him during his last voyage, the windsurfing world lost
a very special figure. Apart from his distance
crossings, the Baron was always at the forefront of
development, here seen piloting one of his own
designs at an early speed trial*

astonishing speed of 38.86 knots on his speed board, beating the previous record held by the catamaran 'Crossbow' by nearly two knots.

Long distance

Despite their size, boards have covered some remarkable distances, thanks more to the bravery, stamina and ingenuity of the pilots than the nature of the craft themselves. In 1982, Frenchman Christian Marty crossed the Atlantic without leaving his board, a feat bettered three years later by his compatriots Frédéric Beauchêne and Thierry Caroni, who completed the same crossing on their tandem without a back-up vessel. Frédéric Beauchêne had already rounded the treacherous Cape Horn in 1979. Englishman Tim Batstone circumnavigated the British Isles in 1984. But undoubtedly the most colourful adventurer of all was Baron Arnaud de Rosnay. His crossings include the Sahara on a 'speedsailor' (a windsurfer with wheels), the Pacific and the Bering Strait from Alaska to Siberia. He promised his beautiful young wife Jenna, herself a windsurfing champion, that his crossing of the Formosa Strait between Taiwan and the People's Republic of China would be his last. Tragically, it was. He set out on 24th November 1984 and disappeared without trace.

Chapter 2 SAILING THEORY

The windsurfer is the purest sailing craft: it does everything because of, and in relation to, the wind. In order to become a proficient windsurfer, you must learn how the wind works on a sail, how it can be harnessed to make the board turn, and how it can limit your possible sailing courses. If you have never thought of it coming from a single direction your first windsurfing sessions may be somewhat confusing. Within a very short time, however, your feel for the wind will become instinctive. You will learn to spot its approach across the water and even be able to anticipate the strength of the gusts. These are essential skills to acquire in order to improve your windsurfing.

Points of sailing

Your first and easiest course of sailing on a windsurfer is at ninety degrees to the wind – a beam reach. From here it is easy to come to terms with balance and basic rig control. For your own safety and enjoyment, however, it is important that you do not become a 'reaching sailor', but learn to steer on all points of the wind so that wherever you are you can always sail back to shore.

Tacking upwind
No sailing craft can sail directly into the wind. In an area roughly forty five degrees either side of the wind direction, the sail stops generating a forward force, flaps impotently, and the board starts to drift backwards. This is known as the 'no-go zone'.

To reach a point directly upwind of your starting point, sail in a straight line on the edge of the no-go zone, close hauled. You then turn the front of the board through the wind (tacking) and take up the same position on the other side before sailing off again. Sail as close to the wind as possible, on the new tack. Like a climber negotiating a steep hill, you should zigzag to your goal.

Tacking or 'beating' is traditionally the novice's stumbling block. It takes considerably longer to make ground upwind than downwind for you have to cover twice the distance. There is also more force in the sail and the board travels slower. In strengthening winds it can be especially difficult, since every time you fall the wind drifts you further away from your goal.

Downwind sailing
Broad reaching is a diagonal downwind course and, in strong winds, is the windsurfer's fastest point of sailing. Sailing directly downwind is called 'running' and, for reasons described later (see Chapter 5), provides a challenge rather than pure enjoyment. Gybing is the other way of changing tack. It is the downwind turn, where the back of the board passes through the eye of the wind.

Apparent wind
There are three winds to take into consideration when windsurfing:
1 The true wind is the wind felt when standing on the beach. The direction will be indicated by windsocks and fluttering flags.
2 The headwind is produced when you move through the air – the wind you feel, for example, if you stick your head out of the window of a moving car on a still day.
3 The apparent wind is the combination of the true wind and the head-

wind. It is the apparent wind you feel when sailing and to which you trim your sail. Its actual direction depends on your speed. As you accelerate, and your headwind increases, it moves forwards, and as you slow down it moves backwards. Imagine a column of smoke blowing at right angles out of the funnel of a stationary ship. When the ship starts to move and creates a headwind, the column of smoke starts to flow backwards. The angle at which it blows indicates the apparent wind direction.

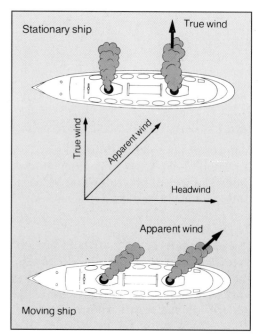

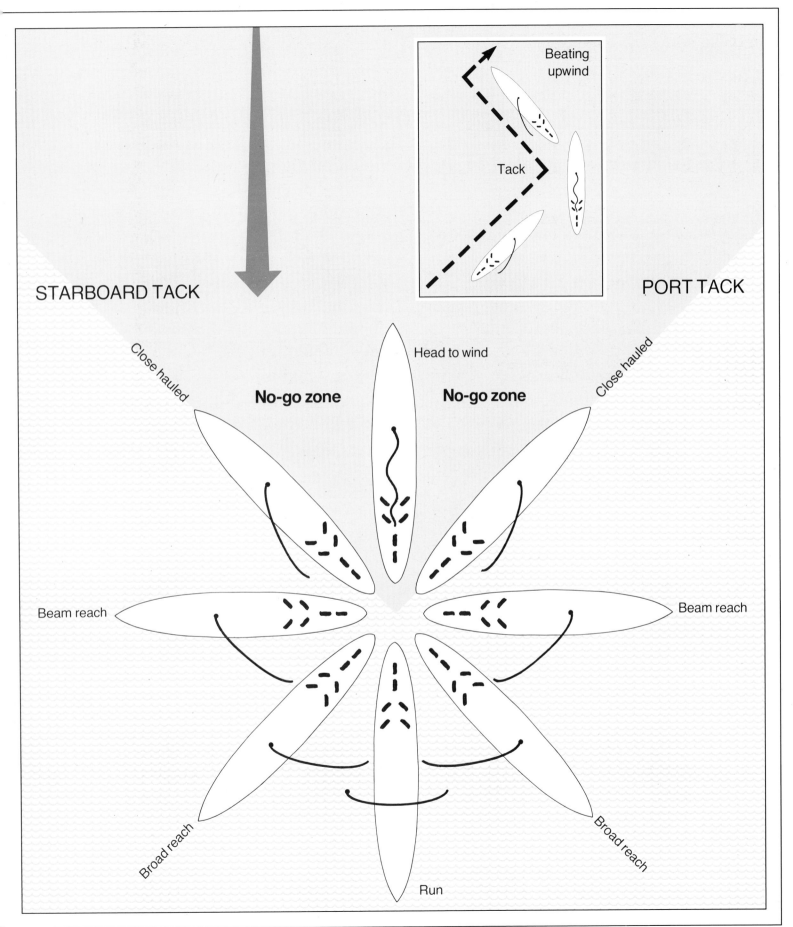

STARBOARD TACK

PORT TACK

Beating
upwind

Tack

Head to wind

Close hauled

Close hauled

No-go zone

No-go zone

Beam reach

Beam reach

Broad reach

Broad reach

Run

How a sail works

It is quite easy to see how a board sails straight downwind. The wind pushes it along like a paper boat. What is less obvious is how the sail manages to drive a board towards or across the wind.

Like an aircraft's wing, a sail is an airfoil. The wind divides when it hits it. The air passing over the leeward side (the side furthest away from the wind) has a longer distance to travel and is forced to accelerate. As a result a pressure differential arises, with high pressure on the windward side and low pressure on the leeward side of the sail. The sail is constantly drawn forwards into the vacuum and consequently, like a wing, generates lift.

Trim angle

For the sail to create this lift, it must be held at the correct angle. Its most efficient position is with the apparent wind striking the sail's chord line (the straight line across the curvature of the sail) at approximately twenty degrees. If this angle is too small and you undersheet, the sail will luff (flap) and the pressures on the two sides of the sail will equalize.

If the angle is too great and you oversheet, the smooth laminar flow over the sail will be disturbed and once again the pressure difference and the lift will be reduced. Therefore, the closer you are sailing to the wind, the more the sail must be sheeted in.

The next question is how can this lift be used to drive the board forwards. Forward motion occurs as a result of lift and a sideways force. The closer the board is sailing to the wind,

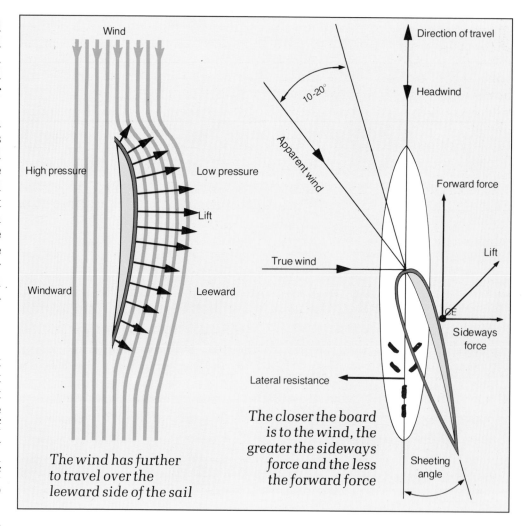

The wind has further to travel over the leeward side of the sail

The closer the board is to the wind, the greater the sideways force and the less the forward force

the greater that sideways force, hence the need for the daggerboard to provide lateral resistance to stop the board drifting to leeward. When close hauled, the sideways force is far greater than the forward force, which explains why upwind sailing is such hard work, especially in a stiff breeze. As you bear away from the wind on to a beam reach or broad reach, the sideways force decreases as the forward one increases, to the extent where, in

planing conditions (force 4 and above), the board's hull and the fin provide all the necessary lateral resistance and the daggerboard can be retracted.

On a run, however, the wind simply hits the sail rather than pass over it. Your speed is therefore limited to that of the wind. On a beam or broad reach, the laminar flow over modern sails is so good that you can travel considerably faster than the wind.

The steering principle

If you lay a board in the water with the daggerboard down, and push either the front or the back, it will revolve. There is a point in the middle, however, over the daggerboard, where you can push as hard as you like and the board will not turn but just drift sideways. That is the board's pivot point or Centre of Lateral Resistance (CLR).

The sail, too, has a central point.

Although lift is created along its entire surface, there is a spot corresponding to an area of maximum camber where all the power is focused – the Centre of Effort (CE).

If the CE lies over the CLR so that the sail's power is acting over the middle of the board, you will sail in a straight line. If, however, the rig is tilted forwards so that the CE lies in front of the CLR, the bow is pushed away from the wind. Conversely, if the rig is tilted backwards so that the CE lies behind the CLR, the stern is pushed away so that the board heads up towards the wind. The board revolves about the centreboard just as if you were pushing the front away with your hands. Remember, the rig will continue to turn up or downwind until the CE is brought back over the CLR.

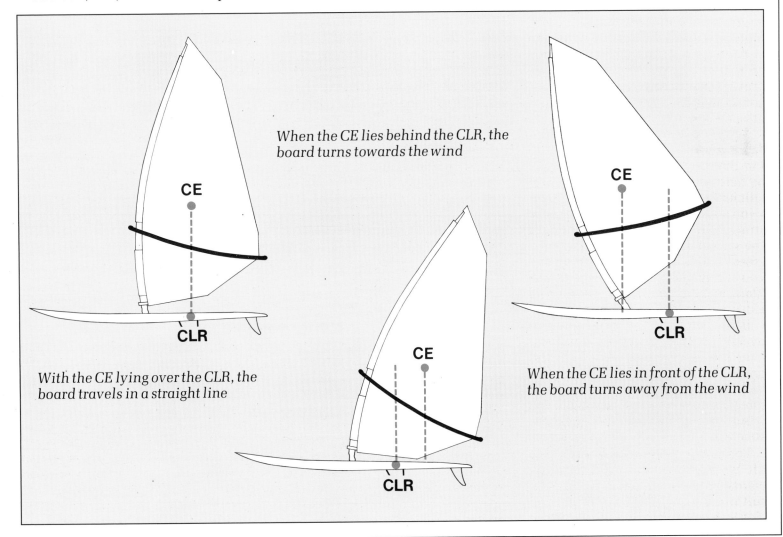

When the CE lies behind the CLR, the board turns towards the wind

With the CE lying over the CLR, the board travels in a straight line

When the CE lies in front of the CLR, the board turns away from the wind

Despite the efforts of those who will have you believe that a full quiver of racing boards and sails is essential before you can enjoy your time on the water, in reality too much can be as detrimental as too little. Having the correct tools is essential and will ultimately decide whether your water sessions are fun and fruitful, or whether you stagnate and fall by the wayside. The selec-

tion process can be quite straightforward, even enjoyable, provided that you take into account your actual standard and the extent of your ambitions, as well as the places you sail and the conditions you are likely to encounter. A skeleton knowledge of how the board, sail and all their components work is vital to the understanding of sailing techniques and helps you make a wise choice.

Board design

Discussing board design in just a few pages is like being dropped in the ocean and trying to paint a picture of it. It is hard to know where to begin. The fact that, given the same brief, two of the world's most respected board builders could produce markedly different designs reveals that we are dealing with an inexact and at the same time fascinating science. The ever-changing wind and water conditions, the sailor's weight, his expertise, the desired performance characteristics are all variables that confront the shaper and make the task of creating 'the perfect board' for all conditions impossible.

A cloud of mystery still covers the shaper's plane. The slightest cut, the smallest channel can turn a good board, under the feet of a wizard, into a great one without anyone quite knowing why. It is known, however, which basic ingredients make a board either fast, manoeuvrable, good upwind, early to plane etc. The shaper's job, therefore, is very much one of compromise, mixing those ingredients in such a way that the board either excels in one area, or performs reasonably well in a wide range of conditions.

While the subtleties of design may escape the near-novice, whose only

comment might be that the little ones are easier to fall off than the big ones, learning to associate certain traits with different levels of performance not only helps clarify elements of technique but ultimately allows you to talk sensibly to a custom shaper and have a board made to your own specifications.

Volume

The bulk of the shaper's energy is devoted to making boards for planing

conditions. His chief concern is to build in features that coax the board on to the plane, or help it perform once it is up there. Volume, however, whether you are buying a first-time board or a sinker, is a crucial consideration. A litre of volume supports a kilogramme of weight. For a board to support you and the rig and sail efficiently in light winds, it should contain approximately 130 litres of reserve volume. People of average weight, therefore, require boards with

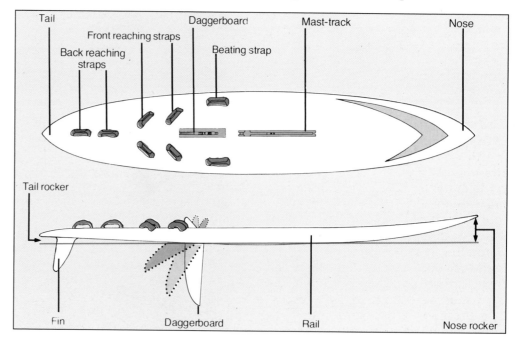

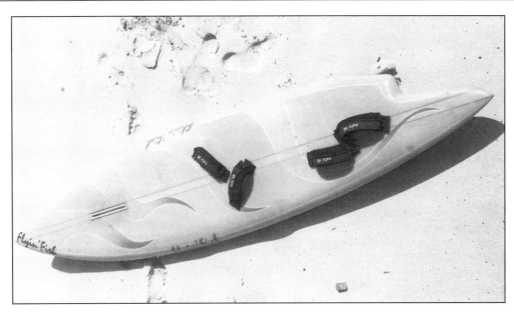

a minimum of 220 litres in total if they are to be happy off the plane.

Buying too small is a common fault all the way down the line and can be equally frustrating in strong winds. The lower the board is in the water under your weight, the more wind and skill you will need to make it get up and go. When selecting a short board, remember that larger people can apply more weight to the turning edge, so are not forced to the ridiculously small to get 'looseness' and manoeuvrability.

As important as the volume itself is the way it is distributed. The board should be thickest under the mastfoot to support the weight and power of the rig, tapering down to a narrower, thinner planing area. Exactly how much volume there is in the tail will determine the board's suitability for different wind strengths. A thick tail, while keeping the board level in light winds and helping it to plane early, will bounce around and become less controllable as the wind increases. A thin tail, meanwhile, sinks in the lulls but stays in the water at speed.

Tail shape

During the funboard revolution, the world was hungry for bizarre tails, in the vain belief that therein lay the secret to super performance. The designers pandered to the fashion with 'double-winged swallows', 'drop-winged thrusters' and many more. Sense finally prevailed as people realized the actual shape was immaterial next to their width and the volume. As discussed above, the wider 'corky' tails promote early planing as well as encouraging tight, pivoty turns and

good liftoff in jumps. Thin, narrow tails lend control at speed and have a wide turning circle. Outline shape is especially important on shorter boards where the tail makes up a greater percentage of the overall length. A long, uninterrupted curve offers the cleanest water flow; for this reason, the classic pintail is the most popular shape in all lengths of board.

Wings are still favoured by some shapers as a means to reduce the tail width sharply over the last eighteen inches in order to combine the performance advantages of the wide and narrow tail.

The ultimate in fine tuning is the asymmetric tail, designed for expert riders who are lucky enough to live in a place where the wind and waves always come from the same direction. The tail features a pintail on one side for long-drawn-out turns at the bottom of the wave, and a wider 'squash' tail on the other for sharp 'cutback' turns on the wave face.

Rocker

The rocker line is the curve or 'scoop' running from nose to tail. It is the most crucial element in board design, as an inch either way totally changes a board's character. Some houses now employ computers to help them find that elusive perfect curve. The rocker's importance lies in the fact that it determines how the board lies in the

water, and how much and exactly what shape the wetted area will be at various stages of acceleration. It decides the drag factor, the board's speed, its manoeuvrability and the manner in which it rides over or slams into the waves.

The theory is quite straightforward: a straight rocker line will promote speed since the board will ride flat in the water with the nose down. A lot of rocker makes for a curved planing area which will 'push' water causing drag. Although slow, that curve also allows the board to pivot on the tail and makes the board highly manoeuvrable.

As you might expect, therefore, long race boards, slalom boards and speed boards have very little rocker, while small wave boards, which need to spin on a sixpence, are bananas by comparison. In practice, however, the solution is not so black-and-white. The current line of thought is that the fastest shape is a very smooth, continuous rocker line which allows the board to rise up on to a continually smaller planing area without the tail digging in. Flat sections disrupt the water flow, so even on race boards, where the rocker appears to be flat from midway to the back, there should be a subtle continuous curve.

A near-perfect way to resolve the dilemma is the 'Tinkler Tail' (named after its inventor). It is spring-loaded

Board design

and flexes when foot pressure is applied, making for a variable rocker line – straight for speed and extreme for the gybes. It is, however, very hard to laminate and therefore costly; furthermore, it is somewhat vulnerable. A stronger alternative is Mistral's bolt-on tail system. The same board arrives with a selection of back ends to suit a variety of sailing conditions.

Rail shapes

The shape of the edges or 'rails' also has a profound effect on the board's speed and turning ability. The basic options are hard (sharp) and soft (rounded).

Hard slab rails are now almost standard issue down the full length of course racing and slalom boards. The long hard edge allows the water to release quickly and cleanly, thereby giving the board lift and reducing the wetted area and the drag. The effect is remarkable in that even through chop, you plane *over* the water, not through it. During the carved turn, the hard edge in front of the back third can grab the water and trip up the board. In general, however, gybes are easier the more speed you have on entry.

Soft rails have the opposite effect. They 'suck' into the water and prevent the board from lifting on to the plane. They were common on many all-round boards as a means to make the board more forgiving. In the wobble stage, sharp edges can be hard on the shins. From the point of view of performance, however, some manufacturers are beginning to realize that slow boards are *not* always easier to

sail, least of all in stronger winds.

The soft rail features positively on short boards as a means to promote more aggressive turns. A typical configuration would be a hard rail for the back third to hold the water, softening out towards the front. The sailor can lean forwards, bank the board right over and engage the whole length of the board in the turn confident that the soft rail will push through the water without catching.

Variations on the theme include bevelled rails where the edge is cut in at an angle to allow the board to rise up on to a secondary planing area.

Concaves

Whether single, double, triple or quattro, concaves are built into a board for the simple purpose of channelling air and water under the hull to lift the board on to the plane and then keep it there. Once only found in longer boards, they are now used subtly in a number of different shapes to increase straight-line speed or give the board a floaty, lively turning characteristic. In high winds and waves,

You do not need a lot of equipment to enjoy windsurfing. Fred Haywood, the first man to break the thirty-knot barrier, displays his impressive quiver at speed week

however, a board with deep concaves is almost impossible to keep on the water. With so much air under the hull, it is prone to skipping out sideways.

Having induced air under the board, the designer has to find a way to expel it and divert it away from the skeg. Such is the purpose of the straight 'V' in the very back part of the board. It also gives the board directional stability and makes the turns more positive. The board can rock easily from rail to rail and, when banked into a turn, a flat surface is presented to the water. The board naturally follows the path of least resistance without levelling out half-way round. The 'V' tends to be subtle on course racing and slalom boards designed for medium winds, but quite pronounced on high-wind wave boards.

Types of board

Boards can be slotted into neat categories according to their length and volume. Whether buying second-hand or new, it is important that you recognize their general performance characteristics, and understand their suitability to the various standards and weights of sailor, so that you can select the right machine for your needs.

The funboard course racer
Formerly known as the Pan Am Cruiser after the funboard competition of the same name, this board is inspired by the course racing discipline of the World Cup, and, in many cases, is an exact replica of a team rider's prototype. Measuring approximately 365cm with a volume between 200 and 250 litres, it is designed to excel on all points of a triangle course in as little as eleven knots of wind. It carries a fully-retractable daggerboard, mast-track and footstraps for both reaching and beating. They are a joy to sail, easy to handle by most standards of sailor and possess an uncanny turn of speed

for their size. The drawback, and there had to be one, is a hefty price tag which reflects the use of exotic composite materials, the high cost of research and development and the limited numbers made.

The all-round funboard
This is a cheaper, heavier, detuned version of the racer, made from a more durable material such as ASA or polyethylene. As its name suggests, it boasts an all-round performance in light and planing conditions, without excelling in any one area. It is a popular choice amongst beginners and intermediates keen to master the basics and progress to stronger winds and funboard techniques.

The mid-length funboard
Measuring 320–340cm, the mid-length funboard is a scaled-down version of the all-round funboard fitted with the same extras – e.g. mast-track and retracting centreboard. It has received criticism over the years, some people suspecting the manufacturers of providing an unnecessary resting

stop on the way down to short boards. For most people of average weight, it does fall into no-man's-land, lacking sufficient volume for a comfortable light-wind performance, yet too long to be manageable in surf. However, the 330 is a convenient size for women and lighter people. It also appeals to committed strong-wind sailors who want to experience the liveliness of a shorter board while remaining secure in the knowledge that they can float home safely should the wind drop.

The 295
The 295 marks the beginning of the short board domain and demands a high level of expertise. The daggerboard has disappeared, indicating that the board has been designed with high-wind reaching and downwind manoeuvres in mind. In fact, the 295 covers a multitude of sins. Some are imitations of slalom boards used in the World Cup – light, very fast, with easy gybing characteristics. Others come in the form of floaty wave boards, and are slower but have the

---

Footstraps
Almost all boards have them; how many depends on the size and type. A long course racing board will have as many as nine, a sinker as few as three. They correspond to the different sailing positions you adopt. There might be a set for beating as well as two sets for moderate and strong wind reaching.

Remember that they are detachable and, since they are usable only in winds above force 4, it is wise to remove them and leave yourself

with an uncluttered deck on which to find your feet and practise the light-wind manoeuvres. When the time comes to brave stronger winds, screw in the lot, find out which ones you use and take off the rest.

Regrettably, even on some of the more exotic brands people have been forced to exchange poor quality straps for sterner stuff. Check these desirable features:
1 Are they easy to adjust without a screwdriver? The best have a simple double velcro fastening system.

2 Do they stand up? There is nothing worse than sulking straps that stick to the deck and need rubber winkle pickers to prise them up. The footstrap cover should be arched and preferably lined with a stiffening material e.g. extruded plastic.
3 Are they comfortable? Some materials blister bare feet after a couple of sailing sessions, namely plastic and nylon. Neoprene strap covers are kindest on the skin. Check that the screws and hard webbing at the base of the straps are also covered.

Course racer and mid-length funboard *Production and custom slalom boards* *Asymmetric and 265cm wave boards*

ability to perform tight, pivoty turns in and around the surf. It is possible to uphaul this length of board in an emergency, but, with a volume of around 110 litres, it is a shaky business. You should consider waterstarting compulsory.

The sinker
So called because it will not support a person's weight when stationary, the 'sinker' is your ticket to the ultimate windsurfing experience. Measuring from 275cm down to 240cm or less, the vast majority are custom-made to suit the individual and conform with the contrasting requirements of wave sailing, speed sailing, speed slalom etc. Although some experts have been seen uphauling their sinkers, it goes without saying that you should be an experienced, fit funboard sailor before attempting to sail one.

The Division II board
Also referred to as the 'displacement' or 'round' board, this is something of a specialist racing machine used in Division II open regattas. Its distinctive canoe-shaped hull actually displaces the water like a dinghy, which, combined with its enormous volume (over 300 litres), gives it a storming light to moderate wind performance.

That same rounded shape also makes it wickedly unstable downwind, one reason, along with its high price and fragile construction (many are hollow), why it is avoided by recreational sailors. However, since a Division II board ousted the Windglider as the Olympic board, the class has made something of a comeback worldwide, and especially in France.

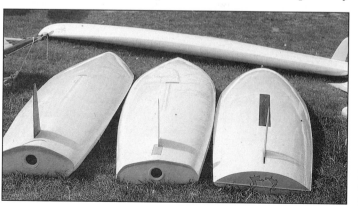

A selection of Division II displacement hulls

24

Daggerboards

Small daggerboards from mid-length recreational funboards and one from Mistral's one design racing board (right) for good upwind performance

Without a fully retractable daggerboard, the long all-round funboard would be neither 'all-round' nor a funboard, for the simple act of rotating or retracting it totally changes its character and its performance in light and strong winds.

When down, the daggerboard balances the sideways forces of the sail to produce a forward vector. For this reason it is something of a necessity when going upwind, since it is then that those sideways forces are greatest. The board itself is naturally more stable at rest and steers conventionally by the fore and aft movement of the rig.

When up, provided there is enough wind, the board will plane on its tail, and steer through foot pressure on the inside edge. In brief, it becomes a funboard.

Retracting plates (which are the same thing) are fitted to most boards longer than 320cm. Sadly, many regard them merely as a lifebuoy, to be used only in an emergency when the wind drops and they have to struggle back to base. However, by choosing to ignore their existence, they are missing out on a valuable source of power, speed and enjoyment.

People cursed the old daggerboard because it rose to the surface in strong winds and capsized the board. On funboards, however, you can use that lift to get the board planing in as little as eight knots of wind. You can control the lift factor by raking the daggerboard back or forwards and by

For a board to footsteer, the daggerboard must retract fully to leave a smooth planing surface

playing it off against the mast-track position. You are effectively juggling with the board's CLR and the sail's CE to find the perfect trim. It is an excellent way of increasing your awareness, your speed and your all-round ability.

Types of daggerboard
The daggerboards themselves vary considerably from board to board. On recreational models, they are generally plastic and too small and too flexible to be efficient. If you want to race or just enjoy going fast upwind, it is worth seeking out a decent plate and checking for certain qualities:

1 A daggerboard is foil-shaped and works on exactly the same principle as a sail, in that the lateral forces set up a pressure difference on the two sides of the foil. The foil's thickness and the position of its widest point determine the lift and the drag factors and the daggerboard's suitability for light and strong winds.

A blunt, thick foil creates lots of lift and is good, therefore, for light winds and slower speeds when the drag is less noticeable.

A narrow foil with its widest point further back has a lower drag factor and is more efficient in strong winds.

2 Stiffness is crucial and is governed by the construction. If the plate twists under the load, the pressures equalize and you lose power. Laminated wood – marine ply, spruce or mahogany – wrapped in fibreglass and epoxy resin is a popular way of making a custom dagger, due to the stiffness, lightness and low friction of the finished product. It is desirable to have a small amount of flex in the tip to absorb sudden surges of power so long as it then resumes its proper shape immediately. In this respect, wood has a better memory than plastic.

3 The size of the daggerboard and the thickness of the foil will be limited by the width and length of the cassette as well as by certain class racing rules, if you intend to compete. You can easily make the dagger wider if you do not mind the trailing edge standing proud of the deck when retracted.

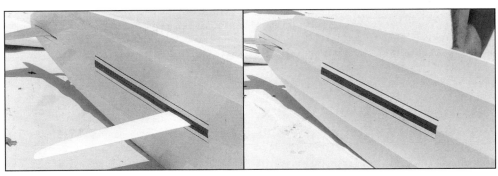

Fins

The fin, or 'skeg' as it is commonly known, like the daggerboard, is a foil which converts the sideways forces of the sail into forward motion. In light winds, it is purely a source of directional stability that prevents the back of the board 'fishtailing' in the water. Its size determines the speed at which a board will steer towards or away from the wind. A racer, for example, may well fit a shortened skeg for light winds to allow him to manoeuvre quickly and gain a tactical advantage.

In strong winds, however, under the feet of an expert funboard sailor, the fin is an essential source of power. Its size, shape and construction dramatically affect the board's speed, gybing characteristics and windward performance. When the daggerboard is retracted and the board is planing, the fin constitutes a significant percentage of the total wetted area. That percentage increases the stronger the wind you are sailing in and the smaller the board you are sailing on, until, in the most extreme circumstances, you are planing solely on the fin.

A fin works in much the same way as a sail. By virtue of its foil shape, the water flows faster over one side than the other, creating a pressure difference and, therefore, lift. The size and shape of the fin, and the thickness and efficiency of the foil section, determine both the lift and the drag factors.

The conflicting demands of speed sailors, wave sailors and course and slalom racers mean there can be no one fin for all occasions. Those desirable qualities of power, lift and manoeuvrability are not wholly compatible. The narrow-based fins suitable for wave sailing, for example, would leave the course racer drifting sideways, unable to sheet in, while a wide, deep-foiled racing fin would make the sinker too stiff in the turns.

Primary features

In fact, no one knows exactly what is going on under the fin. It is subject to so many changing forces and passes through such a variable medium that it is impossible to simulate those forces accurately, despite the most expensive tank testing equipment.

Today's fin designers draw on two chief sources of information:
1 The fins of nature's most efficient swimmers, sharks and dolphins.
2 Aircraft technology and the proven lift and drag characteristics of different shaped foils and wings.

Construction

A fin must be stiff. If it flexes, like a sail twisting or a board bending in the water, it spills power. Mass-produced fins are generally made of moulded plastic. The cheapest bend and are brittle, while the better ones are reinforced with fibreglass, steel or nylon. Ultimately, the best and naturally the most costly solution is the hand-made product. The shaper starts with a sheet of laminated fibreglass or, better still, carbon fibre and grinds it down into the desired shape.

The finished product is guaranteed to be stiff but the smoothness of the foil is due totally to the skill of the individual. It is now accepted that a degree of flex in the tip, as with the daggerboard, is desirable to cope with surges of power, so long as the fin immediately resumes its original shape.

The foil

The thicker the foil, and the nearer the widest point is to the leading edge, the greater the lift and the drag. In many situations early planing and acceleration are more beneficial than a potentially scorching top speed, especially since that speed might be unobtainable due to other factors such as a choppy water surface, lack of wind or the drag factors of the board and sail. Consequently, the majority of fins for general use and even for high-performance sailing have thick foil sections, approximately thirty per cent back from the leading edge. For speed sailing in high winds on flat water, the foil can be much thinner and further back to reduce the lift and minimize drag.

The rake

As we saw with the daggerboard, the angle at which the leading edge meets the water also affects the lift vector. Fins designed for moderate winds will have a rake angle of as little as five or ten degrees (the angle at which the board planes), while wave and high-wind fins are swept back to reduce lift and hold the tail of the board in the water.

Size and width

The equation is simple: the bigger you are, the greater the lateral force you exert on the board, so the bigger the fin you need. A fin which is too big will generate an uncontrollable amount of lift. In the gusts it will start to capsize the board in the same way as a dagger, at which time it is wise to insert something smaller.

Most of the power is generated at

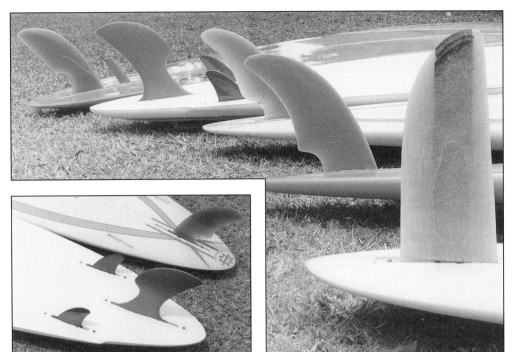

The deeply-foiled course racing fin (main picture, foreground) gives power and lift; the swept-back, cut-away wave fin gives maximum manoeuvrability. The small fore-fin diverts air away from the main fin to prevent spin-out. A single fin and three-fin arrangement (inset). The thrusters reduce speed but provide grip in steeply banked turns

the base of the fin, so powerful fins tend to be wide in this area. Such width, however, increases the board's pivot point in the turns; wave fins, therefore, are considerably narrower in the neck.

Spin-out

Spin-out or 'aeration' occurs when air is sucked down the underside of the board and fills the vacuum on the low pressure side of the fin. When the pressures equalize the fin stands in a pocket of air and loses its grip in the water. The experience is similar to breaking a fin; the back of the board breaks out without warning, leaving you sailing sideways at an impressive rate of knots.

Ragged technique (see Chapter 12) is partly to blame for spin-out, although often the fault lies in a badly constructed, poorly designed fin.

The cut-out

Most contemporary fins feature a cut-out section at the top of the trailing edge. Subtle on race fins, extreme on wave fins, this has the effect of narrowing the neck and gives the air a chance to release before it can travel down the fin. The design does work, although it is generally believed that the cut-out does nothing actually to prevent spin-out but makes recovery from it a great deal easier.

A smooth foil is paramount. Any flat spots, bumps, nicks or abrasions disrupt the water flow, creating turbulence and aerated water.

Fin placement

Your first priority is to fit the fin tightly. If loose, it will vibrate and hum,

and, although the screaming sounds reassuringly fast, it merely signifies a loss of energy and will increase the risk of spin-out. Pack it out with tape until it is solid in the fin box.

In most boards you can adjust your fin about 10cm/4in either way. The exact placement becomes increasingly critical the shorter the board. On long boards, unless you are seeking extra manoeuvrability in sub-planing winds, it is best to place the fin right back in the box. This allows the board to rise on to a smaller planing area and gives you better directional stability in waves and over chop.

On a short board, it is the distance between the skeg and the mastfoot that determines the board's manoeuvrability; the closer they are together, the easier it is for the board to pivot and the looser it feels. Short boards are so sensitive to trim and vary so much in design that you must take a screwdriver to the beach and keep experimenting with the fin placement.

Thrusters

Having once been almost standard on all boards less than 3m, small 'thruster' fins mounted either side of the central fin are now less popular; many riders prefer the faster,

smoother turning characteristics of the single fin. Thrusters cause extra drag and slow you down and, if much bigger than 10cm/4in, can generate enough lift in fast turns to make the board skip and bounce out. However, they offer extra grip when the board is banked over on a wave face, and promote those sharp, snappy turns that are the hallmark of wave riding.

For maximum manoeuvrability, locate them in the back of their boxes with the central fin forwards, thereby shortening the pivot area.

Selecting a fin

'The more we find out, the less we know' is an adage that could easily be applied to fin design: the sometimes extraordinary shapes that confront you in the equipment shop appear to fall in and out of fashion as quickly as the board shorts at the other end of the counter! Gratefully, while some dabble with the fantastic, others stay at the front by using conventional, well-made shapes. Indeed, the fin's outline shape is less significant than its area and the quality of the foil.

As a final word of advice, fitting a cheap fin into an expensive board is as sinful as throwing a Mini engine in the body of a Porsche.

Mast-tracks

Sliding mast-tracks received a mixed reception when they first appeared on production boards. It was a case of people mistrusting what they did not fully understand. Some were confused by the qualifying adjective for no sooner did the thing so much as sniff the sand than it locked solid where it last came to rest, never to 'slide' again.

Although the latest tracks are not totally grit proof, they are now an integral part of the modern funboard and no one doubts that only once you are using the track effectively, can you start to sail the board to its full potential.

With the mast located in one place, your only means of trimming the board for different wind strengths and points of sailing is by moving your feet. Using the track, however, you can alter the mast's position, and therefore the point at which the power of the rig makes contact with the board. By moving it forwards, you increase the board's waterline length and give it better lateral resistance for going upwind. By sliding it back you reduce the wetted area, thereby improving your reaching speed and your manoeuvrability. In marginal winds, you can use the track to trim the board level, stop the nose or tail dragging and encourage it to plane early.

Tracks vary considerably in design. Some locate in a fixed number of positions, others lock as soon as the pedal is released, allowing for infinite adjustment. The release should be a pedal rather than a button, easily operable without having to take your eyes off the sea ahead, and preferably not, as on one unfortunate design, attached to the slider. Reserve the splits for freestyle!

When coming to terms with the basic tacks and gybes, you will not want to use the track, least of all by accident. The better systems have a blocking device with which you can neutralize the pedal and lock the mast in a central position. An explanation of the technique of adjusting the track, on purpose, while sailing, is given in Chapter 12.

On most boards under 290cm, the sliding track is replaced by a skeg box, which allows for some adjustment but not while afloat. The reason for this is that short boards are often used in extreme conditions. The sudden strain placed on the mastfoot landing from a jump, for example, could easily pop a sliding mechanism. Furthermore, the position of the rig on a short board is governed by the position of the skeg and the footstraps and the amount of rocker. You might make minor adjustments on the beach to accommodate a larger or smaller sail but on the water you trim the board just with the feet and toes.

The pedal-operated mast-track allows you to trim your long board while sailing. Slide it back to reduce the wetted area for fast reaches and forwards to increase the board's waterline length for upwind work

The rig

As beautifully conceived and constructed as your sail may be, it will flutter like bloomers in the wind if supported by an unsuitable mast, boom and mast extension.

In the beginning, the nuisance factor has been removed. Your windsurfing package contains a standard rig, which in most cases is perfectly acceptable. It is when you feel the need to add bigger or smaller sails to the collection that problems arise. Masts that are just too short and booms that are just too long will corrugate the sail and make life on the water unnecessarily difficult. Making do with what you have got is false economy.

Your rig should be a solid whole, with each component complementing the other. Compatibility is a far more important factor than expense.

Masts

When selecting a mast for a certain sail, ask yourself the following questions:
1 Is it stiff enough?
2 Does it have the right bending characteristics?
3 Will it be strong enough for the use you will put it to?
4 Is it the right diameter to fit your mast extension, the luff of your sail and/or your inducers?

Stiffness is measured on a numbered scale from one to 10. Most masts register somewhere between 6 and 8, 6 being horribly floppy and 8 being super stiff. As a very general guideline, rotational, recreational sails require a stiffness factor of around 6.8, while induced racing sails need as much as 7.5 – 8.

Mast bend Many make the mistake of believing that a stiffer mast will solve all their creasing problems. Such may be the case if your sail loses shape at the hint of a gust, but as important as the stiffness factor itself is the way in which the mast bends. When the downhaul is tensioned, the mast must conform to the luff curve built into the sail. The sailmaker usually draws the luff curve with certain masts in mind, and it makes sense to select one recommended by the manufacturer.

Strength The mast is your most vulnerable accessory. It is not uncommon for them to break under the strain of being rigged on the beach, while the shorebreak is all too often their graveyard. Although more expensive, it is wise to buy one with a breakage guarantee.

The choices

Alloy/metal masts, being both stiff and light, have been favoured by racers for many years. The straighter luff curve of most racing sails demands a stiffer mast while the weight saving adds to speed and ease of handling. Their major shortcoming is their poor memory. If they bend severely under the load of a breaking wave, they tend to stay bent. For that reason, and the high replacement cost, they are not ideal for wave sailing.

Fibreglass masts generally have neither the stiffness nor the bend of alloy masts but are eminently suitable for the majority of RAF and other high-performance recreational sails. The very best are almost indestructible. The more expensive ones boast carbon strips for extra stiffness and

Light alloy masts are best for racing sails, while tougher fibreglass ones suit wave sails. The two-piece mast (left) is designed for the traveller

strength. Sometimes the strips are used to pre-bend the mast, thereby giving it a dual stiffness factor. If you set the sail against the bend the mast flexes less. It is a sound theory, although sliding the mast up the sleeve against the natural luff curve is hard work.

Carbon and carbon composite masts are a recent addition to the equation. Were it not for the fact that they cost about the same as the rest of the board and rig put together, they might take over completely, combining all the desirable elements of strength, stiffness and lightness.

Two-piece masts are designed for the nomadic windsurfer. Airlines quiver at the sight of full-length spars, indeed the holds on many of the smaller planes are too short to accommodate them. Although the join is a slight weakness and has been known to jam up with grit, it does not disrupt the bend enough to harm the set of the sail. Under normal circumstances, the better ones are just as efficient as a one-piece and even carry the same breakage guarantees.

The rig

Mast extensions

To obtain the maximum performance from your rig, the sail when fully tensioned must be as close to the deck as possible. If that gap is much more than 15cm/6in, the sail will feel top-heavy, you will not be able to 'close the slot' and you may find the boom is too high, even though it is set at the bottom of the cut-out. If, on the other hand, the mast is too short, there will be insufficient downhaul tension, and the sail will be unstable.

An adjustable mast extension is vital if you want more than one sail to fit on the same mast. If the mast is too long for your smallest sail it is quite permissible to cut the top off and use the extension to compensate. This has the added bonus of stiffening the bend.

Beware! The greater the extension, the greater the risk of cracking the base of the mast. As a result, it is not wise to extend a mast much more than 50cm/20in.

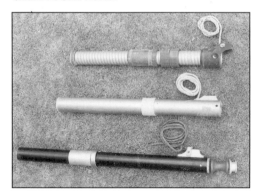

Mast extensions should be adjusted so that the foot of the sail sits as close to the deck as possible. An integral cleat and pulley system is essential for easy downhauling

Booms

From being just two pieces of warped teak lashed together with string, the 'wishbone' as it was then called has developed into an accessory of the highest technology. No longer just a means to hang on to the rig, the boom's quality, or lack of it, can exert as much influence on the rig's overall performance as a floppy mast or a torn sail.

It is vitally important, therefore, to know which is the right shape and length for your sails and which is sufficiently strong for the conditions you intend to challenge.

Construction

Most booms are made of either drawn or extruded aluminium. The actual material used depends to a great extent on how much the tubing is to be bent. The grade of alloy and the wall thickness decide its strength and ultimately its price. In general 17 gauge alloy is for recreational use, with thicker 16 gauge being favoured for booms with surf and heavy wipe-outs in mind. The tubing should be anodized to prevent corrosion and then foam filled to prevent leakage.

The bend

The fickle trends of the early funboard years caused booms to bend in and out like an archer's bow. At first they were narrow not only to complement the flat cut of the sails but also to place you in a more upright stance. In order to accommodate the forward fullness of camber induced and RAF sails and complement the new, upright rig, dropped-bottom sailing

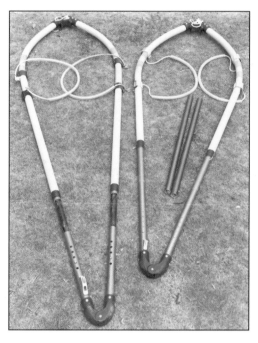

Today's booms have a wide front end to take the sail's forward fullness. These booms have fixed extension pieces and micro-adjustable back ends so that each sail fits exactly

stance, booms have widened considerably at the front end. When selecting one, check that the curve is even since any flat sections denote a weakness. When selecting the bend, you are seeking a compromise between speed and control. The final choice will depend on the sailing discipline it is to be used for; wide is preferable for fast sailing, allowing you to hang more weight to windward, while a narrower boom gives you more direct rig control during tight transitions and places you nearer the centreline in a better position to carve the board up or downwind.

The front and back ends

The front end must have a set of jaws to accommodate the mast tightly and an inhaul system that allows you to get a solid connection. Any movement impairs your rig control.

If the boom has long extensions, a hinged back end is preferable to allow for the change in the bend. It should have a strong yet well-concealed out-haul cleat (cleats mounted on the main body can get in the way of the duck gyber's hand), and an integral roller system.

Adjustables

The ideal solution is to have fixed-length booms for all your sails; however, expense and roof-rack space might forbid such a luxury. The adjustable boom is the most practical alternative. There are two ways of extending a boom; either with telescopic inserts or with fixed extensions. With fewer parts to lose and leave behind, the telescopic boom is more convenient, but any holes drilled into the tubing to house the spring clip do weaken the main body slightly. The fixed extensions are stronger. At the top of the range lies the micro-adjustable, a boom which has both fixed extensions and a telescopic slider at the back end that allows you to make inch-perfect adjustments and lock the clew to the back end. Whichever system you choose, 50cm/20in is the maximum you can extend a boom without dramatically affecting its strength.

Grip

The hard vulcanized rubber around many booms offers such good grip that as your hand turns around, the skin stays in one place. Ravaged, blistered palms can quickly result so opt for a soft rubber covering. This may tear more easily but it is a small price to pay for comfort. Beware of over-thick 'spongy' boom coverings. They are an effort to hold and absorb the energy in your forearms.

Sail design

Once upon a time there were colourful bags. Two decades of experimentation, a host of mistakes, a touch of computer technology and a lot of progressive thinking have transformed those 'bags' into super-efficient airfoils.

The original Windsurfer sail borrowed much from dinghies. The cloth was standard except for the then outrageous colour combinations and the shape was full to the extreme. In light winds the sail worked quite well. Much above a force 3, however, and it was found to be severely lacking. After a couple of windy sessions, the cloth would stretch and ruin the sail's shape. A 'blown out' Windsurfer sail was a common sight around most beaches. A combination of a floppy mast and stretchy cloth meant that the sail's Centre of Effort (CE) wandered aimlessly about the sail in a gust. A comfortable strong-wind stance did not exist. Furthermore, high-wind manoeuvres were made especially difficult by the low aspect design and excessively long boom, the end of which dragged unavoidably in the waves.

The winds of change
The earliest designs were simply variations of the Windsurfer sail.
Step one The leech was hollowed out to reduce the area. Although the boom length remained the same, much of the fullness was removed to make the CE more stable. These flatter, battenless sails went under the name of all-weather or all-round sails.
Step two Booms were shortened and the clew raised to keep the end of the sail clear of the water.

Step three In waves, the clearer air is high up while the early sails had the bulk of their area low down. The most significant move to date was to build out the head of the sail with the use of one or two full-length battens. This not only gave the sail a higher aspect but also encouraged the head to twist open and spill wind in the gusts. These 'fatheads' or 'plumpheads' as they were aptly called were an improvement but tended to work too well in that the enormous head would twist open so much that it caused massive drag. Moreover the whole rig felt top-heavy.
Step four It was the advent of shorter boards that had probably the greatest influence on design. As the early wave sailors pioneered the high-speed carving manoeuvres so widely practised today, power control was of the essence. They demanded sails that afforded them instant forward thrust, without the traditional bending and swaying of spars and booms, and that were quick and easy to flip round in the turns. Moreover, the ferocity of the conditions they were challenging and the gargantuan stresses exerted on a rig by breaking waves necessitated the immediate development of stronger, stiffer masts and booms, and heavier, more stable sail cloths.

It was now more important than ever to stabilize the flow shape of the sails, since a wandering CE atop a short board ensured incurable luffing and spin-out. So instead of simply arranging the panels willy-nilly with extra thickness around the high-stress areas, the sailmakers began to orientate their designs to comple-

The shifting fullness of early sails forced everyone, Graeme Fuller included, into crude sailing stances

ment the stretch characteristics of the cloths they were using.

In Hawaii, for example, Maui sails came up with the vertical cut. They used a softer cloth on the luff to accommodate the different mast bends and help lock the fullness in the front of the sail. Heavier cloths were used around the heavily loaded foot, leech and clew areas. The result was a more efficient and visually exciting rig.
Step five Fully-battened sails had graced the dinghy world for many years. When they finally made an appearance within windsurfing they received a mixed reception. Many believed that the disadvantages – the extra weight, the extra time needed to rig, the extra expense and easily snappable battens – far outweighed the advantages of extra stability, higher aspect and shorter booms.

It was to be that last quality, the shorter boom, that swung the balance. Wave sailing was the talking point and the opinion leaders were starting to perform the craziest manoeuvres right up against the wave face. The full battens allowed the designer to build out the roach and so make even the large sizes fit minute booms.

It was almost a race between the lofts to see who could produce the tallest, skinniest sails. Such a design, however, was found to have very limited application. On the face of a wave, with the wave itself providing the forward motion, it offered maximum control; but on flat water, the tiny boom and the flat cut combined to make a gutless, 'twitchy' sail totally inappropriate for the vast majority of funboard sailors who, bereft of consistent surf, want above all to go fast.

So it was that the sailmakers looked to the growing discipline of speed sailing for inspiration. While the wave sailor, in perfect conditions, demands little power from his rig, the speed sailor expects the maximum drive possible from a given square metre of sail. His brief is to go fast in a straight line down a 500m course and nobody cares much how he turns round and gets back.

A standard rig, it was decided, was not a very efficient airfoil. The leading edge, the round mast, cuts through the wind like a brick and causes turbulence and, with the fullness shifting around in the gusts and disrupting the airflow yet further, the loss of power and efficiency was considerable. This led designers to work on producing a more solid foil, not unlike an aircraft's wing. The deeper the foil, the greater the pressure difference between the leeward and windward sides of the sail and the greater the drive and lift.

The first to convert these theories into practice was Dimitrije Milovich who made the now legendary 'wing' mast which helped American speed sailor Fred Haywood to break the thirty-knot barrier in 1983. The mast itself was elliptical rather than round, was rigid thanks to a carbon fibre con-

struction, and successfully promoted such a clean airflow over both sides of the sail that Haywood was hanging on to a 6m² sail while his rivals struggled to stay with sails a square metre smaller.

However, costing around £1200, the 'wing' was not going to be a favourite with the average recreational sailor. The challenge lay in somehow emulating the aerodynamic qualities of the 'wing' using more standard masts, sails and battens.

The most practical answer was engineered by Barrier Spanier of Neil Pryde Sails with his RAF (Rotating Asymmetrical Foil), an idea copied immediately by all the major sail

manufacturers. Five years later, the rotational is easily still the most widely-used funboard sail. The concept is gloriously simple. The full-length battens slide right past the mast to form a very smooth flow shape on the leeward side of the sail (the side where most of the power is generated). When the sail is tacked or gybed, the luff sleeve rotates and the battens take up the same position on the other side. The desirable shape was achieved by the use of tapered battens which, when tensioned, bend into a foil shape with the maximum fullness, and therefore the CE is locked near the mast.

As with most revolutionary ideas,

Sail design

Gaastra Sail's first camber inducer, which revolutionized sail design and has since been copied by every major sail manufacturer

the RAF was received with mumbles of disapproval. The testers and reviewers stated that such uncompromising power was dangerous in the hands of anyone but an expert. The sail's rigid shape made it hard to trim correctly, hard to de-power and the battens flicked round with such a clunk in the gybes that an unsuspecting public would spend its entire time being flung into the ocean.

They underestimated firstly everyone's desire for speed and, secondly, their ability to adapt their technique to cope with this extra power. Here at last was a sail that fulfilled the needs of all standards of sailor and which did so much to break down that force 4 barrier.

On European beaches where onshore conditions prevail, the sailor needs power to accelerate between the closely-spaced waves and the speed to promote higher, longer jumps. On flat water where sailors tend to specialize in transitions, the greater their speed relative to the wind, the less the apparent power in the rig and the easier it is to relax.

The camber induced sail

Although a step on from the RAF, the camber induced sail now stands as an

Fred Haywood on his way to thirty knots with his Wing rig

alternative rather than a replacement.

The RAF is powerful but it does have shortcomings as the ultimate foil. In gusts, the sleeve tends to rotate back to leave the battens butted up against the mast in the traditional position; moreover, the windward side of the leading edge is not ideal. The camber inducer, nothing more originally than a tuning fork-shaped piece of plastic, stretches out a widened luff sleeve into a 'wing' mast shape and leads the tapered batten right up to the mast. This makes for a yet more powerful rig:

1 The airflow on the windward side is now clean.
2 The foil is deeper and more powerful.
3 The foil is fixed. The sail holds its shape despite fluctuations in wind strength and racers find that they can maintain a constant airflow over the

sail and therefore keep planing even through the lulls.

Today's inducers are considerably more friendly than the first examples. The best rotate smoothly and, thanks to lighter sailcloths and battens, the whole rig feels balanced and manageable. Nevertheless, it should be the type of sail chosen, if not just by the serious racer, then at least by the competent sailor who favours straightline speed in preference to easy manoeuvring. It is certainly not the ideal choice for the sailor who, in the throes of practising new funboard skills, expects to drop the rig frequently. The wide luff tube willingly accepts gallons of water, making the business of waterstarting, and even uphauling, a Herculean task.

Types of sail

Like boards, sails display contrasting handling characteristics. Needless to say, it is essential to recognize the different types and select a design that will complement your level of ability and further your cause.

The soft sail
Far more confusing than the sail itself is the number of names under which this design has been listed. 'Soft', 'fun', 'powerhead' have all been used to describe a sail that carries full battens in the head and foot but which is unsupported in its mid-section except for one or two leech battens. The design is noted for its moderate dimensions and moderate, forgiving handling characteristics. Its ability to luff makes it easy to spill wind in a crisis and there is a definite weight saving over its fully-battened coun-terparts. The last two points have endeared it to many wave sailors who place more value on instant control than power. It does, however, lack stability in strong winds.

The RAF
The Rotating Asymmetrical Foil is the most widely-used sail on wind-surfing waters. It is not ideal for beginners in light winds since it gives no visible signs when either under or oversheeted. In stronger winds, however, the stabilized flow shape makes it powerful and manageable on both long and short boards, provided the sleeve rotates.

The need to de-power suddenly in the most critical situations has endeared the 'soft' sail to wave champions such as Robby Naish

The power and easy handling of the RAF sail make it ideal for most funboard sailors both on flat water and in waves

The extended head of the Cutaway twists open to spill excess wind. The theory is sound but many believe that its appearance will be short-lived

Types of sail

All-powerful camber induced sails being used in a World Cup slalom in San Francisco. Those in search of power, speed and stability have no other choice

The Cutaway

The Cutaway features a negative leech designed to promote extra twist in the head of the sail, the theory being that the greater the sail's ability to twist and spill wind, the wider the range of wind strengths the sail can be used in. Some dismiss the design simply as a marketing ploy, saying that good, traditionally-cut sails promote ample twist. Ultimately, if the sail is well conceived, it will work with or without the cutaway.

The camber induced sail

Aimed initially only at serious course and slalom racers, the camber induced sail is now favoured by anyone, intermediates and experts alike, in search of power and speed. The inducer promotes an even more pronounced and stable foil shape than the RAF, cleaning up the airflow on both the windward and leeward sides of the sail. Disadvantages include unforgiving rotation, a wide luff tube which can trap water and a high price.

The IYRU regatta sail

Division II sailors are obliged to use a sail whose measurements fulfil the International Yacht Racing Union's strict specifications. The maximum size is $6.5m^2$ and the sail is immediately recognizable by its long boom (2.6m) and very low clew. Although unstable in winds above force 4, it is still the most efficient design for light winds.

Long booms abound at the start of a Division II race

Clothing

There are very few locations in the world where it is so warm that you can go windsurfing in windy weather without some kind of protective clothing. No matter the strength of the sun, the cooling effect of wind on wet skin is dramatic; indeed there have been a number of cases of hypothermia in Hawaii. Those who have to brave frosty winters and equally inclement summers must be especially careful, but so long as you are properly dressed, and have the necessary accessories, windsurfing need never be a cold sport.

Wet and drysuits

The three most important qualities of a wet or drysuit are: warmth, comfort and freedom of movement. Thereafter you are free to discuss the year's colours and choose the panel lay-out that shows off the human form in its best light.

In the shop, you are usually faced with a bewildering array of fluorescent designs, but selecting the appropriate garment need not be difficult if you consider your level of expertise and the conditions you are most likely to encounter (light or strong winds etc.), the time of year you intend to practise the sport and, of course, the number and colour of the notes in your pocket.

The two-piece The long-john and bolero top combination is an ever-popular, versatile suit for recreational sailing in late spring, summer and early autumn. On stiller, warmer days, the top can be discarded to leave the shoulders free and put back on when the breeze stiffens and the temperature drops. It is not, however,

Hung on the right frame, the wetsuit has become a fashionable as well as functional accessory

to be recommended for funboard sailing since the open neck lets in a lot of water if you are completely submerged.

The one-piece Funboard sailing is a total immersion sport. Novice or expert, you spend a lot of time in the water. It is, therefore, essential to have a suit that is well sealed at the neck, legs and arms for minimum water penetration. The one-piece 'steamer' is ideal. Its thickness and cut varies according to the season for which it is designed. 5ml rubber is recommended for winter (which often lasts 9 months of the year in northern Europe), while 3ml is sufficient for summer with short, or detachable, sleeves being a comfortable option.

The shortie, with short legs and arms, is reserved for tropical climes, where a thin layer of insulation over the vital organs to guard against wind chill is all that is necessary for a long, warm sailing session. A neoprene surf vest which covers just the trunk is also popular in paradise.

The drysuit in its original form is an impermeable, baggy suit with thin latex seals at the arms, neck and feet. Warmth comes from the thermal underwear, tracksuit, tuxedo, or whatever the sailor happens to be wearing underneath. It is perhaps the warmest option for those bitterly cold, light-wind days on inland water, but is potentially dangerous in high winds and waves on the open sea. It restricts your movement so much that swimming for a lost board is exhaustingly difficult, and were a seal or the suit itself to rip it could quickly fill up with water.

The dry steamer The boundaries between the winter 'steamer' and the contemporary tight-fitting drysuit have become somewhat blurred. The manufacturers recognize that the prefix 'dry' is something of a misnomer since even the best suits will let in a few dribbles if you hit the water hard enough. They have concentrated, therefore, on designing the dry steamer, a suit which incorporates the manoeuvrability of the standard 'steamer', yet retains the latex seals and waterproof zip of the old drysuit. It is excellent for high-wind winter sailing, and whether you select it instead of the winter steamer is purely a matter of personal preference.

Clothing

The fit

Over most parts of the body, your wetsuit should be the tightest garment you have ever worn. Water will collect in any baggy patches around the crutch, bottom, knees etc., weighing you down and impeding your mobility. You must, however, be able to stretch the arms forwards comfortably and adopt the correct windsurfing stance. A generous cut is necessary around the shoulders and sleeves to allow the blood to flow freely to the arms and to give the overworked forearms and biceps room to expand. The better suits use thinner, high-stretch materials in the shoulder and arm panels.

The 5ml drysuit or dry steamer, the 3ml blind-stitched steamer with detachable arms, and the long-john

The materials

Single or double-lined neoprene are the materials used in wetsuit manufacture. Double-lined rubber is laminated on both sides with a nylon-based covering. Although the lining makes the suit more durable, it also absorbs water, causing heat evaporation from the body and reducing the rubber's elasticity. Single-lined neoprene, or 'smooth skin', is warmer, since the water runs straight off it, and more flexible, but it is easily snagged and torn on sharp objects. Many manufacturers use both materials in their suits, the smooth skin over the main part of the body, and the double-lined rubber on the vulnerable areas such as knees and legs.

Stitching

Cheaper suits are sewn together with either an overlocked stitch or a mauser stitch. Both are strong enough in normal use but in both cases the needle completely penetrates the neoprene, leaving hundreds of little holes through which water can penetrate. A good steamer, which is to spend much of its life in the water, should be glued and/or blind stitched. This is a more expensive process: the needle performs a 'cup' stitch, scooping down to join the two halves without leaving any holes. Some manufacturers heat seal the panels.

Hats

Seventy per cent of your body heat is lost through the head, probably more in the case of the thinking windsurfer, so a neoprene hat is a wise addition for the winter months. They are not a popular item. Not only do they make

The neoprene Balaclava helmet and skull cap, necessary, albeit unflattering winter accessories

The horizontal sealed zip on drysuits impairs manoeuvrability around the shoulders but is watertight. The softer wetsuit zip lets in small dribbles, especially around the neck

Neoprene mitts or dry rubber gloves worn over woollen inners come nearest to solving the problem of freezing hands

Steamer boots give warmth and protection at all times of year. Lighter summer shoes give good grip on polished surfaces but must be a tighter fit than the ones above!

you look rather odd, but they also cover the ears and thus affect your balance. If it really is one of those days when any exposed skin turns blue before it dies, then either pursue an indoor sport or try the full-face Balaclava-style rubber helmet. If the air temperature is bearable but the water is cold enough to give you an instant 'ice-cream' headache, a neoprene skull cap, which leaves the ears free, is preferable.

Gloves
Gloves are marginally less popular than hats. There does not seem to be a wholly satisfactory answer. They all reduce your sensitivity to the rig and, in varying degrees, affect your grip on the boom in such a way that the forearms tire rapidly. If the conditions are so good (the temperature notwithstanding) that you have to go out, then

rubber mitts are undoubtedly the warmest. A smart and very cheap alternative, and one that approaches a solution to the overall problem, is to wear large washing-up gloves over woollen inner gloves.

Boots
Some fanatical short board sailors will tell you that boots cut off the electricity that passes between man and machine. Although slightly nauseating, the statement is based on fact. Heavy boots destroy the individuality of your toes and make you stiff in the ankles. You are less sensitive to the board's motion and will find it hard to keep the board trimmed flat.

However, following unfortunate confrontations with sharp mastfeet, skegs, rocks, tin cans etc. the boot may suddenly look very attractive. They not only protect your feet, but

also ward off frostbite and give you a better grip on the board.

So that your sailing performance is not badly affected, avoid the thick-soled, zip-up Wellington type. Select instead a surfer's boot with a stretchy neoprene body and a supple rubber sole. Make sure it fits *tightly* and that any seams are glued or blind stitched to stop it filling up with water.

Hard plastic shoes are a light summer option, but can get ripped off in the shorebreak.

Harnesses

As with most pieces of equipment, the harness has seen enormous change during the formative years. Once just an ill-fitting, rib crushing, perilous device for attaching yourself to the boom, it has flourished into a supportive body-hugging garment, which if used properly not only conserves energy but also greatly improves your potential speed and performance. There exist today numerous designs, each one favouring a certain sailing style. It is important, therefore, to select one that is, above all, comfortable, and which complements your standard and the sailing you intend to do.

The chest harness, having been for many years the only style available, is now almost extinct. Worn like a waistcoat, it offers limited support, and in high winds only your armpits prevent it from riding up over your head. Although its high hook makes it easier to engage the line during the learning stages, it then forces the wearer into an old-fashioned, arched-back stance. It still has a few friends amongst Division II racers who favour a high hook when going upwind as it allows them to keep more of their body weight on the board.

The waist harness is a favourite with short board sailors since it is small, light and allows total freedom of the shoulders and legs. It also rates as a good first-time buy. The hook is low enough to give you the sitting feeling, but not so low that you have to struggle with very long lines. It supports the lower back well enough, but has a tendency to ride up over the rib cage, especially if the owner's chest and stomach are of the same dimensions.

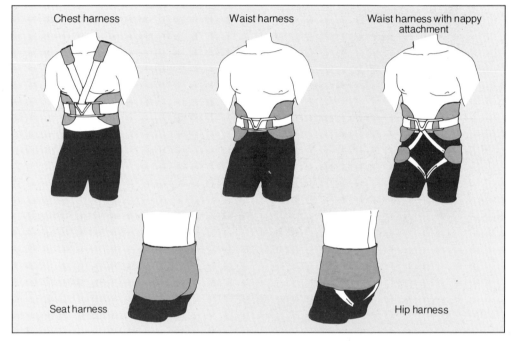

Chest harness   Waist harness   Waist harness with nappy attachment

Seat harness   Hip harness

If such is the case or you feel you would benefit from a lower support, the sling strap or nappy attachment is a useful addition. It is simply a belt that fits under your bottom and attaches to the harness via straps through the spreader bar. As well as spreading the load to the nether regions, it also holds the hook down.

The seat harness is a more substantial version of the waist and nappy attachment, giving total support around the lower back and under the bottom. Its belated arrival on the scene (dinghy sailors had been using a similar style 'trapeze harness' for years) spawned a whole new style of sailing. It was popularized by speed sailors such as Fred Haywood. He set his boom low, used a longer harness to reach the low hook, and then by sitting down he found he could use his body weight to much better effect, support a bigger

rig and go faster. You can happily use the seat as a first-time harness, although you will have to set yourself a high standard of sailing. The low hook is harder to engage, demands that you sail with straight arms and is generally less forgiving. But if used properly it forces you into the correct high-wind stance.

The hip harness is a lighter-weight version of the seat. It is less constricting around the legs and so permits a greater freedom of movement. The harness, true to its name, hangs around the hips and, with a lower hook than the seat, drops your centre of gravity yet further and increases the power potential. The spreader hook itself is not attached to the leg straps and some find that it allows for finer adjustment.

The spreader bar replaced the old single hook which allowed the har-

ness to crush the rib cage in stronger winds. It brought succour to thousands by transferring the load away from the sides, on to the back. It has been modified further to complement modern sailing styles. On some models the hook can slide so that, even when the sailor's body is twisted

forwards when going upwind, he still pulls from his centre of gravity. The fixed tube bars work on a similar principle in that they can move a few inches along the webbing. The hook itself must be wide and 'V'-shaped to prevent the harness line knotting around it in the event of a twisting fall.

The different hook heights of the chest, waist and seat harnesses (left) greatly affect the sailor's stance and his ability to resist the sail's power. Note the varying degrees of bottom and lower back support offered by the three styles shown above

Harness lines

There are a couple of crucial points to remember when selecting harness lines:

1 The rope must be heavy, thick and supple so that it hangs evenly and does not flip round the boom in the wind. Ropes that have been impregnated with resin to make them stiffer tend to twist and kink.

2 Fastening straps at either end of the lines are preferable as they allow for quick, easy adjustment and protect the boom covering. The two main types are the buckle, velcro closure and the 'clinch' system, where the rope tightens around the webbing when weight is applied. Both work well.

The 'clinch' harness line strap is simple to use: it locks as soon as the rope is tensioned. It can, however, jam solid after a lot of use

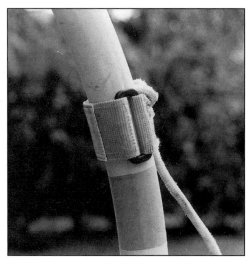

The more elaborate velcro fastening strap spreads the load well and is very easy to adjust

In sport we tend to associate stunning performance with a God-given athletic ability. Champions, we say, assume from birth a champion's role and win whatever the conditions, the state of their equipment and the mood in which they wake in the morning. Robby Naish could win the World Cup sailing a barn door, or could he? Despite a wealth of talent, if his downhaul is slack, if his harness line breaks, if his boom is at the wrong height, if he is stiff from the day before wishing he was still in bed, then he would float swiftly to the back of the pack. Whether you are challenging for World Cup honours or trying to master the waterstart, good preparation is essential.

Rigging

Rigging is the bane of the wind-surfer's life. Wouldn't you like to arrive at the water's edge to find your kit all neatly assembled, ready for use and leave it there at the end of the day for someone else to deal with? And, in your haste to get afloat, don't you rush the job and, casting a blind eye over that frayed inhaul which is bound to last until next time, roughly tension all the corners and be done with it? And, worse still, when you finally hit the water and find that the boom is floppy and the footstraps badly adjusted, don't you tend to soldier on for fear of coming in and missing a minute or two of wind?

Such laziness does so much to hold you back. Once you are familiar with your kit and know your sails' various boom and luff lengths (a job which can be done during non-windsurfing hours), rigging need be no more than a five-minute job. But every extra minute spent 'tweaking' it into shape on the beach, checking the set and the rigidity of fittings and tying-off loose lines, has to be time well spent. Moreover, being on the water with an ensemble that is working efficiently, and which you know will not burst apart, can do wonders for your confidence and this, in turn, can greatly facilitate the learning process.

This sequence shows the process of rigging an RAF fully-battened sail; the order of events is, however, the same for all types of sail. Tuning tips for racing sails are given in Chapter 12

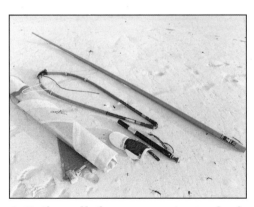

1 Gather all the necessaries and adjust boom and mast extensions to the right length before rigging.

2 Slide the mast up the luff sleeve, fit in the extension and apply light downhaul pressure.

3 Check the boom height by standing the mast upright and measuring it off against your body. For most styles of sailing it should be no higher than shoulder height, preferably a little lower.

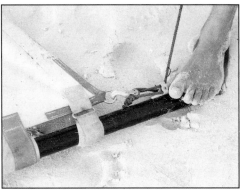

4 There are a multitude of different inhaul systems. Familiarize yourself with yours and then make sure above all else that the boom connection is solid. Any floppiness greatly decreases the direct control you have over the rig. Every movement you make with your hands or arms should immediately make itself felt through the board. Trying to windsurf with a wiggly boom is like trying to play squash with shoes that are three sizes too big.

5 Pull out the outhaul and cleat it off. The flatter the sail at this stage, the easier it will be to tension the downhaul and battens. If you are having trouble pulling it out just using the clew handle, place one foot on the end of the boom for extra purchase.

6 If you are going out in planing conditions, bring on all the downhaul tension you can muster. Your mast extension should be adjusted so that the foot of the sail is as close to the deck of the board as possible. Put one foot on the mastfoot and pull down in line with the cleat. Remember, it is the downhaul tension that locks your CE.

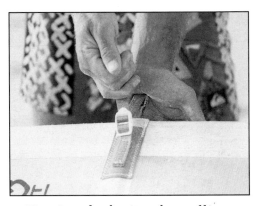

7 Tension the battens by pulling on the strap and pushing in the batten end with the palm. It is only when pushed in hard that the tapered battens bend into the desired foil shape, so be brutal.

8 Release the outhaul slightly to give the sail some camber . . .

9 . . . and if the clew does not quite reach the end of the boom, use the spare outhaul to tie it up to one side. If the end of the sail can move within the boom, the leech will open prematurely, resulting in a loss of power.

Rigging

Dual-batten option

Many rotationals, especially those designed with wave sailing in mind, arrive with a half-batten option. If you feel that the sail is a bit twitchy and unforgiving, try the 'soft mode' by substituting the full-length battens with the two leech battens. It can be especially effective with the smaller sizes of sail ($5m^2$ and less).

A wave sail with a 'soft mode' option (above left). The left-over outhaul line shown above ties the end of the sail to the middle of a boom and prevents any loss of power

Protection

Falling rigs can cause untold damage. It is a wise precaution to protect the rails and the deck of your board by fitting a pad to the base of the mast and a buffer to the end of the boom.

A 'Rad Pad' protects the rails of the board (top) and a boom bumper lessens the chance of the front of the boom burying itself deep into the board's core (bottom)

Rigging tips

1 If it is very windy, standing the mast up to check boom height can be hard work as the sail flaps around and the battens fly out in all directions. A safer method is to lay the rig down and, with your foot in line with the mastfoot, fall into the press-up position parallel to the mast and note where your shoulder is in relation to the sail cut-out. Some people mark the correct position on the mast with a piece of tape; but remember that the exact spot where the boom attaches on the mast will vary according to the sail size and how much mast extension you are using.

2 When a mast breaks, it invariably does so at the boom connection and can often be the result of stress fractures caused when rigging. Yes, your jaws must fit tightly but not to the extent of crushing the mast. If you use the tying method where you attach the boom parallel with the mast before swinging it up or down to take up the slack, do so with caution and listen out for warning creakings. In addition, you might like to try the following:

a. Buy a clip-on, 'anti-crush' mast protector.
b. Reinforce the cut-out area with an extra layer of glass and resin, preferably before cracks start to appear.
c. Some masts are slightly too wide for the jaws, which makes for an unstable, wobbly connection. Do not live with it, but trim down the jaws with a knife.

3 Many people go out with insufficient downhaul tension believing they have done their best with the

Over-zealous inhaul tightening often leads to the mast being crushed within the boom's jaws. A clip-on sleeve offers the necessary protection

A 'wimp stick' in the form of a broom handle or a boom extension is an unlauded means to bring on that extra downhaul tension

muscle power available. There are ways, however, of reducing friction and making better use of your strength to get those extra couple of inches that mark the difference between a stable foil and one that buckles in the gusts.

a. Wet the downhaul rope and the mast before sliding it into the sleeve and pull the rope directly down the line of the cleat, not to one side.
b. Make sure the rope is in no way twisted as it runs from one pulley to the other, and use a system with at least a 4:1 advantage.
c. Find yourself a boom or mast extension or an old length of broom handle, tie a loop (bowline) in the end of the downhaul, slide the loop over it and, with one or both feet against the mastfoot, pull as if in a waterskiing position.

4 The only way to stabilize the original surf sails was to stretch them as flat as a drum. Feeling slightly overpowered, some people have tended to do the same to their RAFs in the knowledge that a flat sail is less powerful than a full one. Right and at the same time *wrong*! By flattening

your RAF you do de-power it, but you also pull the fullness back thereby increasing the power on the back hand and making the sail more twitchy and *less* controllable. When overpowered, either change down or increase your downhaul tension.

Problem diagnosis
Horizontal creases and wandering CE are the result of insufficient downhaul tension. The wind simply blows out the creases and the fullness flows aft.
Vertical creases can usually be removed with more outhaul and/or more batten tension. Do not worry too much about small vertical ripples, as they will disappear when the sail is filled. On soft sails there will be a vertical fold running down the unsupported area next to the luff. *Do not* try to pull this out with outhaul tension – it will fill out into the desired shape once you have sheeted in.
Diagonal creases radiating out from the head towards the clew indicate a mast of the wrong stiffness. In little or no wind, if the creases are near the head the tip of the mast could be too

Rigging

stiff. If they only appear in a blow, it could mean you are simply overpowered, or that the mast is too soft.

Horizontal creases and a floppy cutout signify a severe lack of downhaul tension

To rotate or not to rotate

It is common during the rigging ritual to see a keen, yet frustrated funboard sailor vainly micro-adjusting his every line before thrashing his sail back and forth in order to try to get it to rotate.

Do not be too influenced by what you see in the showroom, where the exhibitor will rig the sail in such a way as to exaggerate the foil effect with the sleeve completely rotated. To achieve this, he applies only moderate downhaul tension, so as not to over-bend the mast. Now, were you to take this sail out in a strong wind, as soon as a gust hit, the mast would bend away, the battens would de-

rotate, the sail would flatten off and the CE would move back.

The truth of the matter is that however you rig your rotational, in strong winds the battens will not remain fully rotated, so you must pre-empt the mast bending in the gusts by applying maximum downhaul tension. The battens will come away from the mast, but the sail will be much more stable and, thanks to the shape cut into the panels and the tapered battens, it will still take on an efficient foil shape.

In sub-planing conditions with the larger sizes, you may ease off the

An RAF rigged for light winds. The battens are fully rotated to promote a smooth airflow on the leeward side

downhaul so that the sleeve can rotate freely. This also encourages the leech to open when you pump the sail.

If you find that the battens are sticking on one tack, in light and strong winds, the problem might be more fundamental:

1 The luff sleeve may be too tight around the mast.
2 The luff may be sticking due to sand or grit. Wash the sleeve and the mast with fresh water.
3 The mast may be too stiff, especially in the tip, and will be trapping the battens.

For strong winds: more downhaul has pre-bent the luff, pulling the battens away from the mast

Sail selection

In order to improve your funboard technique you have to be comfortably powered up. Consider the alternatives: underpowered and the board sits in the water and does not react to footsteering – carve gybing is impossible and waterstarting unnecessarily difficult. Overpowered and you spend the whole session in survival mode, locked in mortal combat with the elements, muscles taut, teeth gritted. Staying on becomes your only goal. You tire very quickly and the board is prone to luffing and spin-out.

'Comfortably powered' for funboard sailing means that the board rises effortlessly on to the plane and once you have reached maximum speed the rig should feel light enough for you to relax and assume a comfortable stance.

The size of sail you take out will depend on a number of variables:

1 Your ability. During the learning stages, a small sail is essential even in light winds. It allows you to recover from awkward positions and is easy to pull out of the water. *Beware*! Staying with an undersized rig for too long breeds lazy, sloppy technique. The more you improve and the faster you can make the board go, the bigger the sail you can handle.

2 The type of sail you are using. Camber induced sails, for example, hold their shape better in the upper wind strengths than soft sails of the same size.

3 The type of sailing you are doing. Racers and speed sailors aim to be on the very limits of control, while wave sailors prefer to be slightly under-

powered for better control on the wave face.

4 The length of board you are using. You can carry a lot more sail on a long funboard than on a sinker. If you were using a 6m² on your 365cm, you would rig a 5m² sail or less for your short board.

5 Your weight, size and strength.

On the beach the best way to resolve the dilemma is to let another decide for you. Look out on the water and note what size someone of similar build and standard is using, and make your selection according to whether he is going backwards, performing endless catapults or looking comfortable.

Should you be the first to arrive, make an educated guess, rig up and then support the rig on the beach in the sailing position. If you can hang against it comfortably then you will almost certainly be underpowered on the water. Given that the apparent force in the sail decreases as the board starts to move forwards, it should be a struggle to lean against the rig on the shore.

Assuming a sailor of average weight (11½ stones for a man) and skill is using an RAF-type sail on a long funboard, here is a rough guide as to which sizes might be appropriate for the different wind strengths:

Force 1–3 (1–10 knots)	6.5m²–7.5m²
	(the biggest in your quiver)
Force 4 (11–16 knots)	5.5m²–6.5m²
Force 5 (17–21 knots)	4.5m²–5.5m²
Force 6 (22–27 knots)	less than 5m²
Force 7 (28–33 knots)	less than 4m²
(it would now be unwise to venture out on a long funboard)	

Racers aim to be on the limits of control and use as big a sail as possible to remain on the plane. Ladies World Champion, Natalie La Lièvre, holds down a 7m² camber induced sail in a force 4 to 5

A final observation is that many people go out under-sailed. Playing safe is, under most circumstances, a responsible attitude but it can be counterproductive if it prevents your board from planing. Remember the following when you are skimming the surface:

1 At speed, the board feels more stable, there is less drag and so less pull in the arms.

2 The funboard manoeuvres are only possible when the board is planing.

Preparing the board

The rig assembled, it is now time for action ... or is it? We tend not to think in terms of 'rigging' the board itself as we rush to the water's edge. After all, there does not appear to be very much that needs attaching or adjusting. Indeed there are only a few points to remember, but taking a couple of minutes to check them out can make all the difference to a day's sailing.

Damage

Damage is not always the result of a head-on confrontation with a breakwater. Little dings (breaks in the skin) can appear unperceived following a rough beaching or a tumble in the surf. The smallest crack in the skin lets in water and the longer it is left unsealed, the greater the chance of a soft spot or possible delamination developing. It is wisest to run a hand over your board immediately *after* a sailing session in order to give yourself a couple of days to dry the board out and repair it in time for the next outing should you find a hole. Imagine the tears of frustration at finding a gaping chasm in the bottom of your beloved board just as you were about to launch into a sunny force 5.

Skeg box

If ever you are demobilized on the best windsurfing day of the year, more often than not it will be thanks to a ripped-out skeg box. Tremendous pressure is exerted on the box in windy conditions, so check the area thoroughly for any signs of movement or stress fractures. Do not try to conceal the gravity of the wound with elastoplast, but take it to an expert who can reinforce the whole area with epoxy, high-density foam and wooden blocks.

Before setting forth, rub down any nicks and abrasions with fine wet and dry sandpaper, and then make sure the fin fits tightly in the box. Re-member, any movement will increase your chances of spinning out and put extra strain on the box.

Footstraps

These must be adjusted correctly for reasons of safety and performance. Velcro fastenings can give a bit during windy sessions, and when you shed your boots for summer and put them back on for winter the strap must be altered accordingly.

The footstraps must fit tightly across the widest part of the foot/boot. You must, for example, have your back foot in far enough to straddle the centreline of the board and therefore be able to trim it flat by depressing the toes. Too tight a fit and all your weight will come to bear on the windward rail, causing incurable luffing problems. The front heel, meanwhile, will drag in the water. Too loose and, as you push against the strap, the windward rail will tend to lift causing skipping and

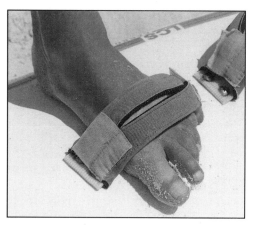

Correctly adjusted. The footstrap fits tightly across the widest part of the foot with the toes over the centreline

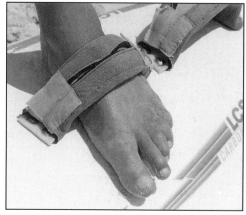

Too loose. The sailor loses direct control over the board and, in a fall, the foot could pass through the strap

Too tight. The foot will tip the board to windward and make it head into the wind

*When board and rig part company in
the surf, the results can be quite
devastating. One wave sailor now
faces a long swim*

spin-out. Worse still, following an acrobatic dismount, you might surface to find the strap up to your knee. The possible consequences of such an action can be left to your imagination.

The daggerboard

The daggerboard must rotate freely. Wash grit and stones out of the cassette and off the plate itself. If it is still sticky, trim down the rotating pins and/or spray the plate with a Teflon or silicon lubricant. The alternative is to buy boots with steel toe caps and practise your football kicks!

The mast-track

This must move easily. Slide it back and forth a few times and, if it sticks, a fresh water douche is usually the cure.

Safety line

Last, and perhaps most importantly, remember at all costs to attach a safety line between the rig and the board. If possible, secure it *above* the UJ (universal joint) in case the UJ itself should break. An unattached board can drift faster than Mark Spitz.

Most windsurfers now have an integral safety line. If it is long enough, the board automatically turns head to wind when the rig releases and remains almost stationary

Physical and mental preparation

However keen the mind, if the body stands inert and unwilling on the shore, the veins empty of red blood and the muscles tired and knotted then the show will lack that verve and dynamism essential for a stunning performance.

It is doubtful whether anyone would dive into a tennis, squash, rugby or football match without some kind of warm-up, not unless they were determined to lose and do themselves serious harm. Why is it then that ninety nine per cent of windsurfers, the pros included, step directly from the changing-room to the footstraps without so much as touching their toes?

Undoubtedly, it is because you are so eager to get sailing that you conveniently dodge any hurdle that obstructs your direct passage to the water. Windsurfing, however, on funboards especially, is a sport and the more keyed up you are physically and mentally, the better your level of performance. Even the most acrobatic skills do not rely on bulk muscle power, but on a certain physical and mental agility. In windsurfing the ever-changing medium holds your attention to such an extent that you do not realize how mobile you are or should be on the board. If the limbs are stiff and slow to react, the board follows its own route.

Warming up
Warming up for windsurfing need not bite far into your sailing time but can become an integral part of your preparation ritual. Your simple warm-up programme could begin in the car. Squeeze a wrist exerciser, or a tennis or squash ball, to warm up the vital forearm muscles with multiple repetitions. Then, on arrival, dressed warmly in comfortable, loose-fitting clothing such as a tracksuit, immediately unload your kit and carry your board down to the water's edge and run back. *Do not* linger around in static mode discussing the weather! It is essential to stimulate the cardiovascular system before sailing so that the specialized muscle groups used for windsurfing are supplied with ample blood. It is unadvisable to break sweat on cold days, as the open pores allow for dramatic loss of body heat, but a sustained 5- to 10-minute effort, either jogging or cycling, followed by a short rest, will place you in an active frame of mind.

Stretching
Although you must be mobile on board with your feet, toes, knees, ankles and arms constantly trimming the board and compensating for

There is no way Hawaiian wave specialist Peter Cabrinha could bend into this dynamic inverted jump unless he was extremely supple and able to stretch

changes in power, some muscle groups are nevertheless static, stressed and liable to tie up very quickly through lactic acid build-up if they are not warmed-up and stretched. Here are some simple exercises to prepare the appropriate body parts:

1 Hanging from a fixed bar with an inverted and overhand grip simulates the windsurfing position almost exactly. By relaxing and remaining in this 'ape' position for a minute or two, the forearms, shoulders and back are all stretched. Follow this with short repetitions of chin-ups, which is identical to pumping a sail.

2 In the absence of a bar, you can warm up the forearm muscles by extending and clenching the fingers as many times as you can in a minute.

3 The knees work constantly when sailing, whether you are clambering back on board after a spill or bending into a carve gybe. Holding the knees with your hands, roll them from side to side, like a snow skier.

Mental preparation

Imagine the scenario: a blustery late autumn day, where you want to go sailing but have trouble removing yourself from a cosy indoor environment to a chilly seaside car park and then into a wetsuit which you know will still be damp and a touch oderous from last time. You make it to the seafront, speedily go through the rigging ritual, your mind flitting between the work you have left unfinished and what you are going to have for supper.

Eventually, you are standing on the shore, board and rig in hand, eyeing the waves which are now dumping carelessly on the shingle bank. You mistime your launch, plough straight into a wall of white water and are pinned to the sea bed. As the water strikes your face you wake from your reverie as if it is only now that you realize you have gone windsurfing. Up until this point, everything seems to take you by surprise. The shingle hurts your feet, the foamy water makes the board unstable, the wind is gusty near the break zone, and the water is cold!

But you know that shingle grinds your soles; you know you have to be light on your feet on the aerated white water; the wind is always gusty inshore; as for the water temperature ... what do you expect in the middle of winter?

In brief, you are, mentally, totally unprepared for the task ahead. Your body is in the water but your thoughts are still in front of the fire. Had you spent a couple of minutes before going out just looking at the break, imagining yourself hitting the first wave, then you would have been out there 'blasting' instead of sitting on the beach with a broken mast, picking pebbles out of your ear.

The words 'mental preparation' have unfortunate connotations. Perhaps you imagine a robotic athlete psyching himself up months or even years before the big event, or a weird sect of Californians, holding hands in a circle, drinking orange juice and chanting hymns. But this is something much more fundamental.

In the car as you approach the sailing spot or while you are rigging up, you can start visualizing your first steps on the water. Imagine yourself launching or uphauling in the chop and then leaning back against the sail and controlling the power. Imagine the feeling of being hit by a gust and then watch yourself sweeping through a perfect gybe. Experience the problems and then try to correct them. Aim to hit the water having already been sailing in your mind's eye, and mentally alert to all possible outcomes.

Chapter 5 CONSOLIDATION

Never was the saying 'Don't run before you can walk' more appropriate than when applied to the windsurfing learning process. There are those who try to leapfrog up the technique ladder missing out as many rungs as possible and, as a result, much of the information and basic grounding essential for the swift learning of the more intricate manoeuvres. There does exist a rare breed of sailor who, with a surfing background, has learned to windsurf on sinkers before heading straight out into the waves. However, were you to place him on a long board on flat water in gusty winds, he may be found to be severely lacking in the fundamental rig control that makes for a good all-round sailor. The importance of mastering the basics becomes manifestly clear when you realize that it is far harder and more time-consuming to 'unlearn' bad habits than it is to learn a new technique properly from scratch.

Carrying your equipment

However ill-disposed you may feel towards your disobedient board, it is a shame to grab it by the scruff of the back strap and drag it mercilessly across the shingle. The designer has already built in the concaves, there is no need to add any of your own.

Irrespective of your bulk, it is possible to lift a long board and rig clear of

Wrong! Heaving your board and rig down the beach in this manner is tiring and does little for their second-hand value

the ground, carry it a considerable distance to the water's edge and still have enough energy to go sailing ... so long as you adhere to the vital concept – let the wind do the work!

You have two choices: either to try to drive the board against the wind, or, to let the wind blow under the assembly and support it free of charge. You can see which option is preferable.

How you actually tackle the carrying problem will depend on a number of variables: the length and weight of the board, the length and weight of

you, how far you have to go and the wind's strength and direction.

Separately
No matter how good your technique, if the board and rig are particularly heavy, their owner especially light and the sea is a long way from the beach, carrying the assembly in two parts is the only answer. The tradi-

The rig carries itself downwind if you hold the mast in front of you at right angles to the wind and allow the wind to blow under the sail

A sound foundation

Until quite recently, the unhappy state of affairs existed where the movements learned as a novice to cope with light winds were irrelevant when it came to attempting to break through the 'force 4 barrier'. It was the shortcomings of the boards and rigs as described in Chapters 1 and 3 that were to blame. So it was that bad techniques (by today's standards) were developed to compensate for bad equipment. Today, however, the excellent standard of the average funboard and rig means that the skills needed to handle strong winds are merely a progression from, not a contradiction to, the basic light-wind techniques.

Whatever stage you are at, near-novice or aspiring wave sailor, it is always beneficial to go out in light winds, inspect the foundations and polish the following most fundamental arts which will then serve you all the way up the ladder of progress:

Stance

How you stand on the board and use your body to harness the forces will ultimately determine whether you tumble at every wavelet or progress to funboard excellence.

Rig control

Rig control is an integral part of stance. The ability to react immediately to subtle changes in pressure in the sail, to cope with sudden gusts, to hold the rig at a comfortable distance and control it during tacks and gybes without a fight becomes increasingly important as the wind strengthens.

Board trim

Keeping the board at its most efficient angle through foot pressure is the key to good speed in light and strong winds. Like a doting mother you must become sensitive to your board's needs, feeling when it is happy and when it is struggling through the water.

Mobility

Good board trim is only possible once you have become mobile on that horribly unstable, disobedient platform. With oiled joints and relaxed muscles, you must find out where you can tread without upsetting the board so that those shaky shuffles progress to positive steps.

tional method of carrying the board with one hand on the daggerboard and the other in the mast-track is quite effective, although it does necessitate an awkward gait. A better method for longer distances is to lift the tail, then work your way up the board so that you can balance it on your head. Walk so that the nose or the tail faces into the wind. Carry the board down first since there is a good chance of it still being there when you come back.

The rig should carry itself. If you are walking into the wind, grab the mast just above the boom with one hand, and the middle of the boom with the other. With the mastfoot facing into the wind, lift the rig above your head and angle it so that the wind can blow under the sail. On breezy days you almost hang-glide down the beach.

Walking downwind, simply hold the sail out in front of you with one hand on the top of the boom and the other on the mast just above or below the boom, whichever feels more balanced. The mast should be roughly at right angles to the wind and, if the sail is fully battened, the battens should be rotated so that the camber faces upwards. Once again, let the wind blow under the sail.

With the back hand holding the dagger and the front hand in the mast-track, you can use both arms to lift the board (left). Hold the rig over your head when walking into the wind, with the mastfoot facing forwards (right). Adjust the angle so that the wind blows under the sail

Carrying your equipment

Together

Carrying the board and rig as one unit is preferable and there are a number of techniques open to you.

Long boards With some of the more robust boards weighing 23kg and more, you may be unable to levitate the whole ensemble.

The shove Initially, if you have a tough recreational board, try lifting the back with the back hand, and, holding the rig to windward by the mast, pushing the board forwards along its rail (provided that the journey is short and the way ahead devoid of rocks). This method cannot be recommended for exotically manufac-

For short distances, stand upwind of your long board, hold the mast with the front hand and the tail with the back, and push the board on its edge

tured race boards, since the slightest obstacle will blunt the sharp edges.

A better method for lighter, more fragile, craft is to stand upwind of the board and rig and with the back hand on top of the boom and the front hand holding the front strap or beating strap. Then bend down and pick the whole lot up, once again allowing the wind to blow under board and rig. Although walking is a little uncomfortable, many sailors prefer this method for both long and short boards since it keeps the board and sail low where it is less likely to be blown around by the wind. You also end up in the water upwind of the board in the perfect beachstarting position.

Short boards present an altogether easier task. Perhaps the most popular method is to stand to windward of the

board and rig, grab the mast with the front hand and the windward front strap with the back hand, bend down and lift. Life is simple walking across or into the wind but tricky when walking downwind since either the sail backwinds or the nose gets blown down into the sand.

The African style of carrying the whole ensemble aloft on top of the head has to be the most effortless, once perfected. Until that time, you are recommended to attempt it only in light winds for should the sail backwind, you can get drilled into the sand with neck-wrenching force. With the mast at right angles to the wind, upwind of the clew, lay the board on top of the sail and tuck the skeg under the boom. To preserve your vertebrae, bend right down, grab a front strap with the front hand and the underside of the boom with the back hand and lift the whole lot over your head, being sure to keep the wind *under* the board and rig. To avoid leaving a head-size imprint on your sail, make sure the board rests directly above your head and takes the weight. You can walk in all directions thus loaded, so long as you swivel the board and rig around to keep the mast roughly at right angles to the wind.

General tips

1 If you are finding it a struggle keeping the board and rig aloft using the above methods, try sliding the mast-track forwards or back to balance them out.

2 All the above methods can be used for long and short boards. The best is the one that feels most comfortable.

By grabbing a front footstrap with the front hand and the top of the boom with the back hand you can lift the lot clear of the ground. This method is sound for all lengths of board especially in strong winds

By holding the rig to windward with the front hand and taking the weight of the sail on your head, walking long distances is more comfortable

Carrying the board and rig on your head is both cool and effortless, but be prudent if you choose this method in strong winds

Uphauling

Uphauling the rig is branded as one of windsurfing's boring necessities, your punishment for falling in. Sadly, lighter men and some women often abandon the unequal struggle with the defeatist words: "I love windsurfing, but I'm just too weak to pull up the rig."

Although it appears nothing more than a feat of strength, uphauling, like all windsurfing manoeuvres, relies more on technique than muscle. Far from being just the novice's starting handle, it will serve you throughout your career when there is not the time, the occasion or the wind to effect a waterstart. It is often the case during a race that you urgently have to heave a huge 7.5m² sail into life after an untimely plunge. And should the wind desert you in mid-ocean on your short board, pulling up the rig, despite your sinking platform, may be the only means of touching base.

Warning!
However slick your waterstarts, whatever the wind strength, no matter how big or small your board, fit an uphaul – you never know when you might need it.

In its simplest form, uphauling in light winds, no matter the breadth of your biceps, is no more tiring than lifting a box of groceries, so long as you obey one or two simple rules:
1 Use your whole body weight to raise the rig.
2 Your leg muscles are stronger than those in your arms, so make them do the hard work.

The disc-slipping position on the left is typified by straight legs and bent arms, while the girl on the right uses her legs and her body weight to raise the sail effortlessly

The upwind recovery
It is rarely possible to perform dismounts so conveniently as to leave the rig lying exactly downwind and at right angles to the board. The exact opposite is more often the case.

Swimming the board into the desired position is *not* the answer. In fact, a neatly executed upwind recovery can be more effortless than the standard method. The key points to remember here are: wind direction, anticipation and mobility.

1 See how the rig is angled in the water and anticipate whether it will swing over the front or the back of the board when lifted up. In this case it is over the back. Now raise the rig gently so that the wind fills on the desired side.
2 It suddenly becomes light, so quickly work your way up the rope until the clew flies clear. Note that the feet are still on the centreline of the board.
3 The rig will swing over quickly so follow it round, being sure to take deft, little steps around the mast with the feet inboard, *not* on the rails. Keep the mast upright and quite close to the body to prevent the clew hitting the water.
4 As the sail swings downwind, it is easy to be pulled off balance to leeward and be forced to drop the sail. Anticipate this by moving your feet swiftly back on to the centreline and by leaning back to windward slightly. Note how the knees have remained bent and the back straight all the way through the manoeuvre for stability.

1

2

3

4

The upwind recovery 1

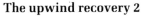

Alternatively . . .

1 A safer, though less adventurous method of recovering the rig from an upwind position, so long as you do not mind which direction the board ends up facing, is to raise the sail a few feet out of the water (as in the first picture of the last sequence).

2 But instead of pulling the clew clear, let the wind blow against the sail with the end of the boom still in the water and push the board around for you.

3 Once you have your back to the wind, pull the sail up the rest of the way. You do not even have to move your feet.

The upwind recovery 2

1

2

Using the wind

The problem with the classic uphaul is that it involves you pulling the rig up *against* the wind so that the more sail you expose, the harder the wind tries to blow it down again – a state of affairs that worsens the stiffer the breeze. Rather than fight the wind, why not make it work for you? It is simply a case of manoeuvring the rig into a position where the mast lies roughly at right angles to the wind so that as soon as the rig is raised just a few inches, the wind can blow under it and lift it up.

3

Getting under way

If you have done a basic course, you may remember the apparently lengthy check list that preceded your sheeting in and setting off: **1** board across the wind; **2** pointing to a goal; **3** drawing the mast across the body etc. When the instructor was looking, you probably followed it religiously but in the knowledge that there had to be short cuts and, as soon as his back was turned, you were going to experiment.

Indeed, there are quicker ways to get going. Strong people in light winds can haul the sail into roughly the right sailing position from just about any angle. A big board in a zephyr is slow to react and forgives such atrocities as oversheeting, protruding buttocks and a buckled back. But as soon as the wind strengthens, the slightest irregularities are spotlighted as the once obedient rig thrashes and tugs like a thing possessed. Remember, the point of refining your technique at this stage is to prepare yourself for the stronger winds.

Bizarre though it may appear, the very simple sequence of movements described below crops up in a host of advanced manoeuvres from setting off in strong winds to aerial gybes. Make it automatic now and save yourself a host of problems later.

Before bringing on the power with the back hand, the basic rule is that both you and the rig should be balanced. The key here once again is anticipation. You know that the sail will try to pull you forwards when you sheet in, so assume a body position that allows you to counteract that force, i.e. with the knees bent, the back straight and your weight committed backwards (to windward), *not*

on your toes. Just try rocking on to your toes on dry land, then bend down and pick up something as light as a basket. Which muscles seem to be working? Most likely those in the ends of your fingers and toes, which are not able to exert much power.

It is a common fault to lean forwards when bringing the power on for fear of falling backwards into the unknown with the rig over your head. But such a fall is less harmful to gear and body than plunging forwards on top of the sail.

In short, success in windsurfing at all levels only comes with total commitment.

1 From the secure position, with the board lying across the wind, select a goal point and place the front hand on the mast below the boom.

2 Now drag the rig across your body to windward until it balances itself. You should be able to see the front of the board through the sail window.

3 At the same time move your front foot back alongside the mast and turn it to face the direction of travel. Now grab the boom about 1m/3ft from the mast with the back hand . . .

4 . . . transfer your front hand to the boom, bring on the power by pulling in the back hand to stop the sail luffing and ease your weight against the rig.

Basic stance

The pen is all too weak an instrument to describe how important it is to refine and perfect your basic stance on the board. During your first forays, much of the time is spent in survival mode. Usually your stance reflects this state of mind as you spread arms and legs down boom and board, tense all muscles and grip with your toes in a forlorn attempt to become a stable, immovable object.

If you soldier on uncorrected, this stance, like anything that is practised, begins to feel normal and almost comfortable. 'Normal' because you have never experienced anything else, and 'comfortable' because you have learned to live with the pain. Although you might start to bring everything together in light wind on flat water, at the hint of a crisis you immediately revert to that primeval pose of your earliest ancestors and so relinquish any hope of moving on.

Strong winds naturally put extra demands on man and machine, forcing you to make certain modifications to your sailing position, but it is important to realize that the basic body postures described below for the light to moderate wind stance are fundamentally the same for sailing the shortest boards in the wildest hurricanes.

Before the gremlins take hold and guarantee you a frustrating future, run the following check down the length of your body:

The head looks over the front shoulder forwards and to windward, to spot approaching vessels/solid objects and gusts.

The hands hold the boom no more than shoulder-width apart, equidis-

Windsurfing is effortless with a good basic stance – head looking forwards, arms straight, upper body parallel to the boom, feet and hands no more than shoulder-width apart

tant from the balance point so that there is equal pressure on both arms.

The arms remain just slightly bent in light winds.

The shoulders should be roughly parallel with the boom, twisted forwards slightly to face the direction of travel. This allows you to straighten out the back arm.

The back must be straight.

The bottom in light winds is tucked in

but not so that the back is arched.

The legs The front leg remains straight, although never stiff, with the back leg slightly bent.

The feet in light to moderate winds should be no more than shoulder-width apart. The front foot is placed alongside or just behind the mast, facing diagonally forwards, while the back foot straddles the centreline, also facing slightly forwards.

Once you know what you are trying to achieve, it is quite easy to refine your own stance since there are a host of physical and visual signs that indicate good technique or betray a need for adjustment. Ask yourself the following questions:

1 Are you in spasm? Muscular agony is a sure sign that one part of the body is overworked due to poor posture. Check hand position and shoulder angle.

2 Do you feel balanced and relaxed? Ideally your centre of gravity should be pulling directly against the CE of the sail. If you are fighting to stay upright with the feeling that you are forever on the point of tipping to leeward or to windward, then check that your feet are on the centreline and that your sail is sheeted at the right angle.

3 Is everyone going faster than you? If so, you have probably either oversheeted or are allowing the sail to luff, thereby losing power. Both problems can be traced back to a cramped, hunched upper body position.

4 Are your calf muscles rock solid? Then stop gripping with your toes! Straighten up, relax the legs and try to hang your whole body weight against the sail.

Power control

Were the wind a constant force, then this next section would be redundant. But equally on sheltered lakes and the open sea, it blows neither steadily nor consistently from the same point. Yachts and dinghies absorb most of these fluctuations through a slight tilting of the hull; the windsurfer, however, must immediately trim his sail and his stance or risk serious upset.

Power control is not a thing that happens naturally from day one; you might remember how your initial reactions to lulls and gusts were exactly the wrong ones – hanging on for grim death when pulled forwards and throwing the sail away when falling back. However, it is only once you are able to control the power, in a variety of situations both in the water and on the board, that you can entertain

thoughts of beachstarts, waterstarts and high-speed funboard sailing.

Sheeting in and out
Sheeting in and out is the easiest method of holding your balance. When sailing along, try to think of your front hand as a hinge about which the sail pivots. The back hand is the means to open and close the door and show out unwanted persons/wind. The analogy is useful in that it helps you remember that it is always the back hand that releases or sheets out when you want to spill power. But do not take it to the extreme of locking the front hand rigid; it must remain mobile and ready to pull the rig back up into the balance position should it drop to leeward.

Anticipation!
The above method is an essential weapon in your armoury, but if you are consistently sheeting out in relatively tame winds, it might be the symptom of deeper problems:
1 Over-cautiousness and fear of leaning your body against the rig to windward.
2 Errors of stance, with perhaps the feet off the centreline, the mast hanging to leeward or the hands not far enough down the boom.

Remember that every time you sheet out and lose power, you slow down. Your aim now is to cope with fluctuations in wind strength by altering your body position while keeping the power on. This is only possible if you are able to spot the gusts and lulls on the water and *anticipate* their effect. In short, get them before they get you!

1 In most instances you can avoid dropping the rig by spilling the wind. If a gust pulls you off balance, *do not* try to heave the rig upright . . .
2 . . . but release or sheet out with the back hand.
3 Pull the rig into the balance position with the front hand and straighten the back before sheeting in again.

Steering

Having learned to steer slowly and predictably in light winds by moving the rig towards either the front or the back of the board, you can very quickly learn to make the board respond quicker by foot pressure. Like the rig itself, the feet apply pressure on either side of the board's pivot point – the daggerboard. By weighting the back foot, for example, you can push the back of the board away as well as encourage it to pivot on its tail. Conversely, you can kick the nose downwind with the front foot, in both cases combining the transfer of weight with the appropriate rig motion.

In stiffer breezes it is important to rely more on foot pressure and less on rig movement to change direction, since any forward or backward movement of the sail is met with a violent change of pressure in either the back or front arm. As with all stronger wind manoeuvres, you must assume a more dynamic body posture and remain mobile, always ready to transfer weight.

Keep the daggerboard down at this stage, the mast-track neutrally positioned and aim to practise the following manoeuvres in a wind strength of force 2 to 3.

Steering towards the wind

1 To practise steering towards the wind, sail off on a beam or broad reach with the daggerboard down and then select a goal point upwind of your present course.

2 Now lean the rig towards the back of the board by extending the back arm. Accelerate the turn by depressing the leeward rail and weighting the back foot. Once the board has turned on to its new course . . .

3 . . . bring the rig back upright and sheet in until the sail stops luffing. If you have to pull the boom across the centreline to fill the sail, you have entered the 'no-go zone' and will soon be sailing backwards; in which case either bear away or assume the secure position and start again.

Bearing away on to a run

Due to the fact that the CE of the sail flows back when the sail is loaded, boards turn more naturally towards the wind than away from it in a strengthening breeze, especially when the dagger is down. There seem to be a number of forces working against you: the daggerboard tries to capsize the board to windward as you accelerate downwind; and the rig tries to catapult you as you lean it forwards.

Everything is possible if you dwell on these essential points:

1 Anticipate the sudden surge in the sail, by bending the knees and keeping your centre of gravity back on the board.
2 Despite the lifting forces of the daggerboard, trim the board flat by pushing hard with the front foot.

1 In light airs leave the dagger down. On a beam reach, lean the rig forwards by extending the front arm and sheeting in with the back arm. Bend the knees and trim the board flat by applying pressure to the front foot.

2 As the board turns downwind, sheet out so that the sail is at right angles to it, slide your hands to the middle of the boom and place the feet either side of the centreline, facing the front about ½m/1½ft behind the mast.

Nevin Sayre bears away around the windward mark during a windy World Cup course race before retracting his daggerboard and pulling back his mast-track in preparation for the reaching leg

Running

It is a mystery why early windsurfing man ever learned to sail dead downwind. It is not a thing that windsurfers do naturally. Running is not only the slowest, most inefficient point of sailing but also the least stable. With the wind simply hitting the sail in paper-boat fashion and not passing over it, it is impossible to sail any faster than the wind; and, with no lateral force against which to balance yourself and with both feet off the centreline, you are supremely vulnerable. In an age when the modern planing hull performs so magnificently on the reaches, why bother running at all? The following answers have been reached after long deliberation:

1 If you compete in Division I, Division II or any Olympic triangle racing, you have to negotiate a running leg.

2 On any type of board, in a strong tide and a failing wind, you may have to sail dead downwind to make any headway and reach your starting point.

3 Running sharpens your balance and your rig control considerably. Division II sailors, who handle their horribly unstable displacement boards downwind over a choppy sea in strong wind, are some of the fittest and most agile of all.

4 The complete windsurfer must be able to sail on all points of sailing.

To a great extent running is a static balancing act which calls on controlled, sensitive shifts of body weight. Imagine trying to balance on a log; sudden movements are disastrous as you automatically over-compensate with an equally sudden movement in the other direction. The movements get bigger and bigger until eventually you drop off.

Shouting 'relax' to someone struggling on a run is a bit like saying 'stay calm' to the occupants of a plummeting aircraft. The advice is good, but unrealistic. On a run, however, you must remain loose about the knees, ankles and waist, absorbing the waves and the changes in pressure with gentle movements of the lower body. Take heed of the following:

1 Stand well forwards, near the mastfoot over the point of maximum buoyancy. This allows the board to ride flat and increases your speed. Of course, in stronger winds you are forced to move back, but not too far. If you sink the tail and cause drag, the pressure in the sail will greatly increase.

2 Stand with the feet comfortably apart (eighteen inches) equidistant from the centreline. If you want to move up or down the board, move both feet together, or bring them right on board before taking the steps.

3 With your arms quite straight, maintain a good distance between your body and the rig to allow for quick adjustment.

4 If your equilibrium deserts you with boring regularity, try sailing a few degrees off true, with the sail angled slightly clew first. This provides a lateral counterbalance.

5 In waves, stay mobile. Although foot movement tends to upset the lateral trim on a run, you must anticipate the effect of the waves and shift your weight accordingly, moving forwards to force the nose down the face, moving back as you hit the trough to prevent it 'ploughing'.

Steering on a run
The run is not a fixed course. You can quickly alter course to the left or right through foot and rig pressure. As well as being an essential tactical weapon on the race course, it is also an excellent preparatory exercise for the flare and carve gybes.

To change direction on a run, use a rig scooping action combined with opposite rail steering. To turn left, the sailor scoops the rig to the right and depresses the right edge of the board and vice versa to steer right. The wider the rig action, the further back he stands on the board and the more he sinks the tail, the tighter the turn he is able to make

The flare gybe

Think for a moment of the gybe in its most basic form. On a reach you release the back hand, take hold of the mast and swing the rig over the front of the board. The board turns downwind with the tail of the board passing through the wind. You change your feet into their new positions and sail off in the normal way – a more satisfying way of changing direction than the tack (see pages 66–7), since the board maintains its speed.

The 'flare' gybe is simply a speeded-up version that relies on a more precise and powerful rig action and positive foot pressure. The turn is initiated by a violent scooping of the rig to windward, which creates a turning moment about the board's CLR, which, if in its down position, will be the daggerboard. The turn is accelerated further by the sailor sinking the tail and engaging the windward (outside) rail.

For many years it was a popular and impressive freestyle stunt, 'flare' being the term used to describe the spectacular sinking of the tail and lifting of the nose that are the turn's trademark. Today it survives in many forms, not least because it is the quickest way to gybe a board with the daggerboard down. Some foolishly brand it as an intermediate manoeuvre and choose to ignore it in favour of the faster, more fashionable, carve gybe. It is, however, a vital weapon in your armoury and one that serves the very best in all winds on all lengths of board.

The advantages
1 Before a race, you will have your daggerboard down in preparation for the first beat upwind. The ability to spin the board quickly on its tail (tacking may send you over the line prematurely) means you can confidently manoeuvre into the smallest gaps, flee the pack and gain an advantage.
2 The dramatic 'slam' gybe (see Chapter 8), although performed on a short board without a dagger, demands exactly the same rig 'scoop' action as the flare gybe.
3 Often is the case during a carve gybe that the wind deserts you in mid-arc, forcing you either to revert quickly to the flare gybe rig action to power you through the last half of the turn, or stall and sink.

Practice
Practise the flare gybe with the dagger down and the mast-track located forwards of centre, in about 6–10 knots of wind (force 3). In winds above force 4 the lift generated by the dagger and the speed of the rotation can make life difficult. Footstraps are not necessary, in fact a clear deck is a positive advantage during the first attempts.

Problems?
Heading back up into the wind as you try to move back on the board is caused by one of two things: either sheeting out, or allowing the board to follow its natural tendency to rail up to windward. You must endeavour to stay sheeted in and keep pressing the windward rail down as you move back on the board.
Over-rotation signifies a failure to move quickly back up the board as it turns through the wind. Also, having scooped the sail, you must fight to pull it back upright *before* releasing the back hand to flip the rig.
Loss of balance is usually caused by lack of body angulation. In the flare gybe the knees must push to the outside of the turn in order to engage the windward rail, while the upper body leans to the inside to resist the pull in the sail. You must remain supple at the waist. Steering on a run (see page 63) is the best way to practise and get used to this motion.

Variations
In stronger winds you have to control the board's speed in order to complete a successful flare gybe. If you let it accelerate downwind, the daggerboard will hydroplane immediately, capsizing the board and sending it into the wind. Only bear away very slightly, therefore, before jumping straight to the back and sinking the tail which will then act as a brake. Control the turn entirely through delicate foot pressure for only the slightest scoop of the rig is necessary to send the board spinning like a top. Having slowed the board down so much, there will naturally be a lot of power in the rig, so *stay low*.

In light winds, jumping right to the back can bring the board to a standstill. Moreover, the turn looks clumsy as you fight to get forwards again to avoid sinking. Try, therefore, to keep the board flatter and accelerate the turn with a wider scoop action. It helps to move the hands down the boom, or even release one hand altogether so that the rig swings right round and almost touches the water to windward.

1 Sailing on a close reach, bear the board away by throwing the rig forwards and to windward, sheeting in hard and pushing with the front foot to keep the board flat.

2 Once on a broad reach, start to move back down the board and stay sheeted in. See how the back foot is placed across the centreline and manages to trim the board level as the front foot moves back.

3 With both feet right on the tail of the board, weight the outside foot and engage the windward rail, maintaining a low position with both knees bent. At the same time, scoop the rig to windward.

4 The board should now spin very quickly. Sheet out into the clew first position as the board turns through the wind. See how the sailor starts to lean forwards, takes his weight on the boom and prepares to sweep his front foot forwards in order to level the board out and kill the turn. As the board turns through the wind, there is a surge of power in the front of the sail by the mast. Anticipate this by leaning the upper body to the inside, keeping the back straight and the knees bent.

5 On the new reach/broad reach, move the front foot forwards, hold the rig away from the body at arm's length and without lingering in the unstable clew first position...

6 ... release the back hand and grab the mast below the boom. Let the sail rotate, draw the rig over to the balance point in the normal way, sheet in firmly with the new back hand and bring the front hand on to the boom.

The tack

Within your first few hours, you probably learned to turn the board through the wind on to the new tack simply by holding the mast or uphaul and leaning the rig to the front or the back of the board. The method worked and your confidence grew in the knowledge that you could sail back whence you came. But you probably did not relish the prospect of turning round as you were forced to relinquish your secure sailing position and set out on that long, lonesome and risky trail around the front of the mast.

The basic tack is a convenience manoeuvre but it is not a lot of fun. You are vulnerable whenever you have no power in the sail and especially vulnerable when you have your

Mast technique
The uphaul rope is an indispensable accessory but its use, as its name suggests, should be limited to hauling up the rig. People do, however, in times of crisis, hang on to it like a lifeline and use it for support during a variety of manoeuvres, especially tacks and gybes. The message is simple. During the starting procedure and during all rig manoeuvres when the sail is being flipped, hold the depowered rig by the mast as it swings round, *not* by the uphaul. The mast is a solid point of contact and gives you positive control over the rig, while the uphaul gives the rig free rein to flap wildly.

feet off the centreline of the board. The basic tack places you in that very situation for what seems like an age. Your aim, as soon as you have basic rig control, must be to speed up the tack, lessen the wobble time, and maintain board speed to the point where it becomes a dynamic and enjoyable manoeuvre.

As with most manoeuvres, you can break the tack down into three parts, the approach, the transition and the getaway:

1 The approach To maintain speed, sail the board into the 'no-go zone', through the wind, so that you are already heading on your new course before you go around the mast.

2 The transition To reduce the time you spend de-powered, aim to jump

1 Sail the board into the wind, by drawing the rig back, weighting the back foot and engaging the leeward rail, sheeting in as the board heads up.

2 As the board approaches the eye of the wind, transfer the front hand to the mast, just below the boom. Note the extended arms which keep the rig at a manageable distance from the body.

3 The back hand continues to sheet in until the nose of the board has passed through the wind, which will be when the end of the boom is pulled across the centreline and the foot of the sail rubs against the shin of your back leg. See how the head is still looking forwards to watch the wind and waves and how the weight is brought inboard and more on to the front foot in anticipation of the jump.

around the mast and land with both feet on the centreline in your sailing position on the new tack.

3 The getaway *Do not* let the board stop; it is far more stable when moving, so immediately throw the mast forwards and to windward to allow you to sheet in and accelerate without delay.

Practise the jump tack on a big board in winds of about force 3. Much less and the board reacts reluctantly to foot pressure and there is not enough power in the sail against which to throw yourself following the jump phase.

Problems?

Problems encountered during the jump tack usually occur during the airborne and landing stages of the manoeuvre. Do not gauge the success of a jump tack by the height of the jump! In fact, the higher the jump, the more you upset the trim of the board and the greater the chance of the two of you parting company.

The jump should be subtle, even in the form of two quick steps, but never move the front foot first so that you are straddling the mast – the consequences could be too painful to contemplate!

Losing the rig to leeward is simply a case of not holding it upright over the centreline during the approach and the jump phases. Make sure you transfer it into your new front hand early, from where it will be easy to control.

4 Quickly transfer the mast to your new front hand, then spring off your back foot, holding the mast upright (in the lateral plane) still at arm's length from the body...

5 ... and land with your back foot well down the board just in front of the daggerboard, on the centreline and with the front foot alongside the mast. Simultaneously, draw the rig into the balance position with the front hand and put the back hand on the boom in its normal place.

6 Move the front hand on to the boom and sheet in hard, bending the knees to counteract the surge of power in the sail. Keep the rig well forwards at this stage in order to bear away and pick up speed.

Chapter 6 **LEARNING TO LEARN**

Learning psychology is an aspect of all sports that should never be overlooked. A confident, fearless outlook is often all that is needed to overcome the most daunting of tasks. Windsurfing manoeuvres are rarely intrinsically difficult, yet it is all too easy to let fear and uncertainty impose barriers that prevent the body from functioning normally. Ultimately, your mental approach to learning has an equal if not greater bearing on your progress than latent athletic ability. Remember, windsurfing is easy if you believe it is, and realistic goal-setting can put you on the road to success.

The inner game

In the last decade a totally new approach to learning has been developed. The Inner Game theory was conceived in the United States and has since almost revolutionized coaching methods, proving beneficial in a number of sports, especially tennis and skiing. It works on the basic concept that you do not have to teach your body anything. It knows how to serve, play a forehand, carve a turn, ride a bicycle, so long as *you* do not interfere.

The theory is exemplified by the child's ability to perform 'naturally', without coaching, complicated physical skills. If you strap skis to his feet and say "follow me", he will. His instinct tells him which ski to weight in order to turn. Why, therefore, do so many adults, infinitely fitter and stronger than a three-year-old, experience so much difficulty? Because as we age, our minds become over-analytical, we develop egos, a sense of self-preservation, in short we become afraid – afraid of hurting ourselves, afraid of making a fool of ourselves, and afraid of failure. All these emotions induce nervous tension, prevent the body acting intuitively and ultimately block the learning process.

A complete Inner Windsurfing programme has yet to be structured and one is left to wonder how effective it would be. Anyone who learned by themselves will remember the endless wasted hours trying to work out what can quite easily be taught in a few minutes on a simulator. However, there are elements of the inner game that are undeniably helpful.

The little voices
Have you ever listened to yourself windsurf? Not to the howling wind or the lapping water, but to that monotonous commentator in the back of your head who follows your every move. The one who expresses all your self-doubts, reminds you what happened last time you tried that manoeuvre, and who can tell you in the split second before you lean into a carve gybe that should you injure yourself, you will lose your job, miss the mortgage repayment, the kids will have to move school etc. Nor does his ceaseless banter stop once you have left the water. He is forever on hand to remind you that you are really too weak/old/sedentary to master any of those fast funboard manoeuvres and should retire to the pond where people of your limited ability and physical make-up live out their days.

There is no one body movement during even the fastest funboard manoeuvres that calls on an unnatural feat of balance or suppleness. If you can bend your knees, you can carve gybe.

Mastering the skills, however, relies on you conditioning your body to co-ordinate a certain set of movements, which itself is achieved by structured practice sessions and realistic goal-setting.

Goal-setting
Four years before the Olympics he was four seconds off the pace in the 100 metres backstroke, an impossible time to make up over such a short distance in a relatively short space of time. Many would have admitted an early defeat. American John Neighbour, however, viewed his apparently insurmountable target in a different light. Four seconds in four years represented just one second a year, less than one-tenth of a second every month. He finally worked out that he would have to improve his time by only 100th of a second every training session to become world champion. He set himself a number of tiny and easily achievable goals which concealed the enormity of the final ambition and became the proud owner of an Olympic gold medal.

Breaking it down
The same condition faces the improving windsurfer. Imagine, during your inaugural session, a short board sailor aerial gybing right in front of you and the instructor telling you that

Fear of falling backwards forces novices into the classic Turkish toilet position

Like the lavatory position, this hips-forward, arched-back stance is uncomfortable. Recognize discomfort as a positive indication of poor technique

within twelve months you would be doing the same thing. Given your present state of competence, the notion would appear preposterous. But if you focused your attention on the present, saying that by next week you would be jump tacking, the week after you would start to use your feet to speed up the gybes, the week after you would try retracting the daggerboard on the reaches etc., slowly you would arrive at the stage where the aerial gybe, far from being a circus trick, would be just the next logical step forwards.

The same building block approach should be used when learning apparently 'difficult' manoeuvres. Take the duck gybe for example. If you were to go out cold and give it a go, your chances of success would be minimal. Your body has no feeling for the manoeuvre. Your movements are stilted and jerky since no part of the body has a clear idea what it is sup-

posed to be doing. Instead, you break it down, starting first with the rig change. Either on the beach or on a long board in light winds, you practise ducking under the sail and throwing it back. When the wind returns, you would perform a series of carve gybes concentrating on describing a long fast arc, bending the knees forwards to lower the body position and releasing the rig early. Then you could try the real thing, only this time, when your mind says duck, the hands and knees automatically know what to do and where to go.

Success and failure

Morale is a fragile phenomenon and has an enormous bearing on your ability to digest new information. You must create a mood of success so that your body expects to stay dry. Such is the advantage of breaking down the skills into easily achievable stages. Ideally, you are not so much

learning a completely new manoeuvre as adapting skills already perfected into a new context. In the furore of a high-wind funboard session, however, the body can quickly become conditioned to failure. You are practising your gybes around a buoy but fall in every time at the same spot just before the rig change. Very soon that bear away-carve-splash routine will be written into the programme. At that stage the learning curve plummets as enjoyment and expectation are replaced by frustration and fatigue. Before you become stuck in that failure rut, you must move on to something else and let time heal a few scars before trying again with a fresh approach.

Experimentation and analysis

Having been encouraged to let your body work automatically, you should now try thinking your way through the manoeuvres. It is not as contradictory as it sounds. Honing certain skills is only possible if you can feel how the board is working beneath you and if you experiment with the most subtle changes of pressure. When settled into an upwind stance, for example, you should try shifting weight from the board to the rig to alter the heeling angle and try moving your feet a few inches along the rail to see if the board finds another gear or just sticks to the water. During fast manoeuvres, try concentrating on one element as a form of diversion therapy. For example, during a carve gybe concentrate solely on how much weight you are applying to the back foot. You may be surprised to discover that as you bear away and push both knees forwards, you develop a habit of leaning quite heavily on the front foot, thereby immediately increasing the waterline length and causing the board to 'stick' downwind. On all funboards, where trim is so crucial to performance, you should always be experimenting with foot placement and pressure.

Analysis
Analysis is a very good substitute for anger following a sudden loss of equilibrium. If after twenty minutes in the waterstart position, you have done nothing but spin into the wind the moment you tried to get on, it is fair to assume that you are doing something fundamentally wrong. At this stage you would be wise to pause and consider before fatigue washes away all hope of logical thought. Once on dry land, you will quickly recall that luffing in beach and waterstarts is a result of insufficient mastfoot pressure. When you try again, you have a specific aim in mind and can alter your stance accordingly.

The idea of structuring your time on the water smacks of the military and appears to exclude the fun element of windsurfing. There is, however, more fun and satisfaction to be gained from perfecting a new skill than from reaching up and down as if on rails. The extent of your 'structure' might just be to experiment using longer harness lines or tighten the radius of your gybes. Learn to recognize when you are not performing at your best and either have a rest or move on to something else before you get frustrated. Above all, make your time on the water fresh and interesting.

Copying the masters
Only a limited amount can be learned from written or verbal instructions. In the majority of situations there is no substitute for watching or sailing alongside an expert and using him as a mirror. Sometimes, however, it is necessary to filter what you see as champions tend to develop highly individual styles. Robby Naish, for example, even in moderate winds, adopts a unique stance with his feet very close together right at the back of the board. It is only uncanny sensitivity and trim that allow him to stand over the skeg and maintain control. A lesser sailor would spin out immediately. Stefan van den Berg, meanwhile, sails with his harness hook facing upwards. Although it is presumptuous to argue with the World Course Racing Champion, there is little to recommend this quirk. Hooking in feels awkward (although obviously not to him!) and the line will not immediately drop out in an emergency if you sheet in.

Visualization
Visualization is a means of fooling your body that you have successfully completed a totally new manoeuvre a hundred times before. Having studied a video or a photo or watched an expert in action, you have a mental picture of the finished article. It is then a case of replaying it over and over in your mind, putting yourself in the driving seat. It is another way to condition yourself to the feeling of success. Before a regatta, some competitors will play the whole race over in their minds and imagine themselves in the lead and the sound of the boards lapping behind them, so that on the water they are prepared to cope with the pressure.

The barriers
Irrespective of your ardent desire to improve, there are certain obstacles, all of them avoidable, which instantly freeze the learning process.
Fear If you were cornered in a dark haunted house by a mad axeman and someone asked you to add two and two, you would probably be unable to answer. You know the solution but due to the hostile environment you are unable to think of anything else but staying alive. A similar situation arises on a windsurfer when you overestimate your ability to cope with certain conditions. Having reached a

good standard on the reservoir, for example, you decide to practise carve gybing on the sea. Out in the wind and the waves, however, you are preoccupied with other matters: Will I be washed up on to the rocks? Is the tide taking me out to sea? Was that a plastic bag or a shark? Recalling the fundamental teaching theory of Safety – Enjoyment – Learning will reveal that you feel decidedly vulnerable, you are not having fun and you are certainly *not* learning to carve gybe.

Knowing your limitations and choosing a location which complements your ability and in which you feel safe are paramount if you are to improve. From the point of view of technique, learning certain skills is very hard in some wind and sea conditions. Gybing is especially hard on choppy water. Beachstarting is positively dangerous where the waves are dumping on to a steeply shelving beach. It takes experience to launch a short board in direct onshore winds.

Waiting a few hours for the tide to drop or driving up the road to a beach with a more favourable wind direction will end up making you a far better and happier windsurfer.

Tuition
There is something of the pioneer in everyone which prevents them from naturally seeking advice from an expert. Certainly it is very satisfying to work things out for yourself. In a windsurfing context, however, that often means immense frustration and the repetition of the same bad habits.

There is a teaching system today that will lead you from beginner to expert in a safe, controlled environ-

ment. Most important is that the instructor can lay the foundations that allow you to progress and will make you aware of your level of ability. It may be your one aim to waterstart and, whereas by yourself you would have drunk half the ocean during your efforts, the instructor would immediately spot a flaw in your basic stance which is making that same goal unobtainable. There is so much that we *cannot* see in ourselves. The right word from a watchful tutor can transform your life in a day.

Tuition is not just for beginners. A word from an expert can save hours of fruitless effort at all levels. Here the instructor checks the stance of a funboard pupil on the simulator before a water session

Given the size and frailty of a board and rig and the extreme conditions in which many can now venture out, it is amazing that there have been so few fatal accidents involving windsurfers. Although national training schemes stress the safety aspect from day one, the very notion that windsurfing might be remotely dangerous somehow contradicts the sport's 'fun' image and is conveniently swept under the carpet by the sales people. Regrettably, it often takes a frightening incident before people switch on to safety. Be prepared and learn to recognize the potential dangers.

Preventive medicine

The worthiest safety measure of all is never to open yourself up to danger in the first place. That does not necessarily mean limiting your sailing to force 2 winds on a tiny gravel pit patrolled by a fleet of rescue boats. Indeed, you could be sailing off the deserted beaches of a remote island in mast-high waves yet still be safe. Forewarned is forearmed in windsurfing. If you are aware of all the factors that might provoke a crisis, it is very easy to take evasive action.

Jenna de Rosnay at a speed trial in Weymouth. Only in a controlled environment such as this is it safe to go out in offshore winds

The elements

The weather, around most parts of the globe, is very fickle. Within minutes, a change in wind direction and strength can turn a friendly sailing area into a cauldron of foam. Before leaving home, therefore, it is essential to obtain a local weather forecast, to discover if there will be enough wind to windsurf at all, and also to find out the direction and whether it is likely to increase, decrease or swing round during the day. You do not have to be a meteorological wizard to windsurf, but a basic forecasting knowledge is very useful as it helps you to interpret in more detail the sometimes rather general national TV and radio forecasts. You are naturally at a great advantage if you can read the cloud patterns and spot approaching fronts and squalls.

The offshore wind is always worth a special mention. It is treacherous. Broken up by buildings, beach huts, trees etc., the wind is light and gusty inshore and, combined with the beautifully calm sea, appears to offer an ideal training ground. However, that gentle force 1 can be a fierce force 5 by the time it has cleared the obstacles. With your back to the beach, you drift unwittingly away from the shore into a wind band which is suddenly uncomfortably strong. Every time you fall, you are blown further out until finally you are left exhausted and panic-stricken, unable to cope with the long, tiring beat back to base.

Given man's compelling desire to get afloat, it is perhaps unrealistic to say *never* go out in offshore winds but at least make sure of at least one of the following:

1 That you are in a controlled situation, in a race for example, where there is ample rescue cover.
2 That you are sailing in a shallow bay or harbour where you are not out of your depth some way from the shore.
3 That there is a near and safe lee shore to catch you.

Lack of foresight and respect for the conditions can land even the very best in dire straits. Ken Winner and Arnaud de Rosnay attempted to race across the English Channel without a support vessel only to run into a force-8 gale a few miles out to sea. Their trip ended aboard the coastguard's helicopter

Tides

Next to offshore winds, the tide is the windsurfer's greatest hazard. It is caused by the gravitational pull of the moon and, to a lesser extent, the sun. When they are opposed we get the small neap tides and when they are pulling in the same direction we get 'springs'. The tide varies all over the coastline and can completely change the character of a sailing location within a few hours. Generally, the tide ebbs and flows once in a twelve-hour period. The two phenomena in question are the tide which describes the vertical rise and fall of the sea between high and low water, and the tidal stream which describes the horizontal flow of the water.

The tide itself is dangerous only insofar as spiky objects which are exposed at low water can be partially or completely covered at high tide. A flooding tide can also cut off your access point if you have launched in front of a sea wall, and can cause the waves to dump on a steeply shelving beach.

The tidal stream can be ferociously strong, up to ten knots in some parts of the world. The speed and direction of the flow depends on the shape and depth of the sea bed and the contour of the coastline. Generally it flows parallel to the shore, but where it encounters a deep water channel at the mouth of an estuary for example, it speeds up and can flow directly out to sea.

The subject of tides is a book in itself. Around the UK coastline alone, there are double tides, tides which rise for seven hours and fall for five, and tides which come in faster than a galloping horse. Your safety, therefore, relies very much on gathering local knowledge and taking heed of the following essential points:

1 The tide flows fastest during the third and fourth hours.

2 If you are sailing at a new location, ask a local about the tidal patterns and which areas and states of tide to avoid. Buy a local tide table (available at garages and newsagents).

3 If you are unsure of the direction of flow, marker buoys will leave a wake and moored boats face into the tide. If no such indicators are present, select an object on the shore and sail a straight course towards it. You will quickly be able to tell if the tide is pushing you up or down the beach.

4 If you are apprehensive about sea sailing, stay close to the shore where the tidal stream is generally weakest. Above all, avoid channels and shipping lanes.

5 Wind against the tide can affect the windsurfer both positively and adversely. In some instances it creates a very choppy and confused sea state. Moreover, if the wind is weak and the tide strong and ebbing, you risk being taken out to sea. On the other hand, in good planing conditions, the tide can act like an upwind conveyor belt and allows the funboard sailor to gybe and broad reach all day and stay in the same place.

Basic rights of way

The more popular sailing locations are becoming so crowded that you can be in more danger from other windsurfers than the conditions themselves. You must be familiar with the rules of the road if collisions are to be avoided.

1 Port gives way to starboard. If the wind is coming from your starboard side (right side), you are on starboard tack and have right of way over someone on port tack. You are on starboard tack when your front hand is your right hand.

2 Windward stays clear of leeward. When two boards are on the same tack, the upwind (windward) board must stay clear of the downwind (leeward) board.

3 The overtaking board keeps clear.

4 In waves, the windsurfer coming in on a wave must stay clear of the one going out through the waves.

5 Make your intentions clear; if in doubt, keep out of everyone's way!

You and your equipment

A great number of rescues are the result of equipment failure. If your board breaks in half or your mast snaps, there is not a great deal, you may think, that could have been done to prevent it. In many cases this is true. However, unless you are sailing in breaking waves, equipment often gives some kind of warning before it disintegrates, usually in the form of tiny stress fractures. As mentioned in Chapter 4, you should check all your gear before leaving the beach, taking special care to replace ropes that show the slightest sign of wear and making absolutely certain you have a substantial safety line attaching the board to the rig.

Clothing
You must wear a wetsuit to suit the conditions. It is much easier to cool down than to warm up so play safe, especially if you are practising a total immersion manoeuvre.
Buoyancy is a controversial subject within windsurfing circles. Many water authorities insist that everyone wears a fixed amount of buoyancy although there is no proof that the new style, non-buoyant waist and seat harnesses have put the windsurfer in any danger. Ultimately it is a matter of personal choice. If you are unsure of your water competence, then wear a buoyancy aid. Wet and drysuits have some inherent floatation and, in normal situations, you fall very close to your board, the biggest buoyancy aid of all. Funboard and wave sailors tend to regard the buoyancy aid as a means to restrict freedom of movement both on and off the board. Swimming long distances

after a lost board in the surf is actually more difficult and ducking under the waves is impossible. Remember that a buoyancy aid is just a swimming aid and will *not* float you the right way up should you be knocked unconscious. Only a fully-inflated lifejacket will keep your head clear and is far too restrictive to be practical for windsurfing.

Spare equipment
There is no limit to the spare equipment you could carry with you. But assuming you want to enjoy the outing and not sink under the weight of a full rucksack, it is wise to think through every possible predicament and then take the bare essentials either in your harness pocket or a separate light-weight 'bumbag'.
Spare rope is indispensable and can be used to overcome a number of crises. It replaces broken inhauls, outhauls, harness lines etc.; it can also be used to lash the mast to the track should the UJ or any other part of the mastfoot snap, and is a means to tow or be towed.
Flags and flares are the most convenient instruments for drawing attention to yourself when lost at sea. A dayglo flag will fold into the size of a postage stamp, while a flare, provided that it is in date and you are familiar with the operating instructions, is the more effective option in heavy seas.

The human factor
Ultimately we are our own worst enemies and, although we may choose to blame our tools for our mistakes, more often than not it is a drastic error of judgment that lands us in danger.

As well as being a confidence booster, a neat buoyancy aid is a great help to the novice waterstarter

In windsurfing, lack of experience or common sense can give rise to the following problems:
1 An underestimation of the ferocity of the conditions.
2 An overestimation of ability. The sudden transition from flat inland water to heaving ocean can turn the confident intermediate into a floundering novice.
3 An overestimation of physical strength and fitness. In heavy weather on the sea, you have to work harder to stay upright. You fall more frequently and tire more quickly. Logic, competence and balance all disappear with exhaustion.
4 Venturing too far out to sea. Unless you are doing a planned crossing, it is rarely necessary to sail further than two hundred yards from the beach. The real enjoyment of funboard sailing lies in manoeuvring and playing in the waves close to shore.

When all fails

It may well happen that you get a forecast, check your gear, assess the conditions, do all that is asked of you but still find yourself faced by an unforeseen set of circumstances that leaves you unable to sail back to land.

The self-rescue
If the crisis has been provoked by the conditions rather than gear failure, the crucial factor is admitting to yourself that you are in trouble. You must stop, stow the rig and paddle home before repeated falls and start attempts leave you too tired to do anything.

The standard self-rescue procedure is effective over short distances in moderate conditions, although paddling a low-volume board against strong wind and waves can be a lot more difficult than sailing.

It is possible to use this method (shown below) on sinkers if the wind drops. Due to the distribution of volume, it is easier to paddle them with the tail facing forwards.

1 Sit astride the board and unplug the mastfoot.

2 Take out the battens and stick them up the luff tube.

3 Undo the outhaul and swing the boom up parallel with the mast.

4 Roll the sail up tightly from the foot.

5 Use the uphaul rope to bind it together and clip it back on itself.

6 Lay the rig on the board with the mastfoot facing forwards and then, either kneeling or lying on top, paddle back to shore.

When all fails

A quicker method if you are left becalmed on a long board is to leave the rig plugged in, rest the boom on the back of the board so that the sail is clear of the water, lie on top and paddle away.

If you have been caught out with too big a sail, you can make quick, controlled progress across the wind by partially uphauling the rig so that the end of the boom remains in the water. The sail will fill and drive you along.

Should you get overpowered, partially raise the rig so that the end of the boom stays in the water. The sail will fill and drive you across the wind back to shore

Paddling is quicker than sailing in zero wind so long as you keep the rig clear of the water by resting the boom on the back of the board

The last resort

The most dire predicaments arise in heavy weather when something breaks or you find that you are suddenly incapable of sailing in the worsening conditions. Unless the wind is directly onshore, any time spent in the water will result in you being swept further downwind of your goal – potentially disastrous if the wind is offshore. As mentioned, paddling an unstable funboard and rig against a strong wind and big waves is very hard work. Let us consider the options open to you.

Swim? If you abandon your board, you abandon your liferaft and are completely at the mercy of the elements.

Throw away the rig and paddle the board home? It is true that the rig, especially on a short board, makes paddling all the more difficult, but in

The international distress signal is to cross your arms repeatedly over your head. If you just wave, your potential rescuers may just wave back!

the majority of cases it is wise to hang on to it:

1 When in the water, it acts like a sea anchor and slows down the rate at which you drift.

2 It is colourful and therefore visible. From the air, that is the part your rescuers will be most likely to see.

3 It is possible that the foul conditions were the result of a squall and could moderate suddenly, allowing you to set sail again.

There are rare occasions, however, when ditching the rig is a sensible alternative. If, for example, you are quite close to shore and sudden gear failure has left you capsized in a strong outgoing current, you might find yourself a long way out to sea by the time you have dismantled the rig. There is a basic rule which governs this course of action: if you ditch the rig, you must be 100 per cent sure that you can make it to the shore.

Sit on the board, draw attention to yourself and wait for help to arrive? If you are injured or have been caught out by the weather, *do not* be a victim of your pride but seek outside help immediately. Use your flare, dayglo flag or the international distress signal (arms crossed repeatedly above the head) in order to make your position quite clear to other windsurfers or sailing vessels. If you have chosen your sailing area well, help will soon be forthcoming.

Being rescued is not good for the self-esteem; but having a battered ego is better than being a proud castaway

Windsurfing need never be dangerous so long as you use your common sense and abide by some simple rules:

1 Will your equipment hold together and are you properly dressed for the prevailing conditions?

2 Get a local forecast and choose your sailing area wisely. Avoid offshore winds, strong tides and currents, and poor visibility.

3 Never sail alone and tell someone on dry land where you are going and when you expect to return.

4 Learn to assess your ability and get to know your limitations. If you are afraid for a moment that you might not be able to handle the conditions, *do not* go out, but look for a calmer location.

5 Be aware of other water users. Windsurfers are very manoeuvrable and should keep out of the way of larger vessels and respect those — ferries, fishermen etc. — who rely on the sea for their living.

Chapter 8 FUNBOARD TECHNIQUES

Funboard sailing is the point at which windsurfing becomes an athletic endeavour rather than a beach pastime. It begins in winds of force 4, when the board will rise on to the plane and adhere to a different set of steering rules. With everything happening that much faster, you are asked to approach the manoeuvres instinctively, controlling and channelling your aggression into explosive moments of action, all the time using the wind, letting it work for you, never fighting against it. Funboard techniques can be learned through good preparation, on and off the water, by breaking the skills down into digestible parts in order to build your confidence. Forging through into this advanced stage of windsurfing calls for commitment, positive thinking, a deep understanding of your equipment, and good basic technique. Thus armed, beach-starting, waterstarting and carve gybing are just a few hours' practice away.

Funboard sailing – the key points

Force 4 is the minimum wind strength needed to push a board on to the plane. It is the time at which the board starts to behave less like a windsurfer and more like a surfboard. Indeed, the most fundamental difference between basic light-wind windsurfing and funboard sailing is that in the former you steer with the rig and in the latter you steer with the feet and use the shape of the board combined with its own speed to drive it round the corners. Although you use your feet to accelerate the turn in the fast tack and the flare gybe, it is rig power pulling around a central pivot point – the daggerboard – which causes the board to turn.

By contrast, for all the principal funboard techniques, the dagger-board, if one is fitted, is retracted. Without the lift and drag factors of the plate, the board can plane on a smaller area and becomes immediately more controllable at speed in high winds. With the skeg now as the pivot point, the board turns on its tail. The turns are, therefore, initiated by depressing the inside rail in much the same way as the surfer banks his surfboard and the skier his ski to force the cutting edge to grip the terrain. In ess-

ence, the 'carved' turn is a far simpler concept. You lean right to go right and left to go left.

Unfortunately, a force 4 and a funboard do not automatically turn you into a planing windsurfer. The disadvantage of having a board that is both fast and manoeuvrable is that it is very sensitive to trim. In fact, despite ample wind and the very best design of hull and sail, it is very easy to make a funboard *not* plane if you

tread carelessly about its deck and channel the power through the wrong points.

None of the exciting carving manoeuvres are possible unless the board is planing freely and, although 'funboard technique' traditionally evokes the image of the most radical manoeuvres on the shortest of boards, your priority must be to learn how to coax your board effortlessly on to the plane and survive comfortably in

Like the surfer and the skier, the funboard sailor banks his instrument into the turn. He uses both the knees and the ankles to maintain his balance and to control the direction of the turn

Raphael Salles captures the spirit of funboard sailing as he commits himself totally to the gybe in a World Cup slalom

strong winds for long periods – a feat made possible only by good stance and harness technique.

You have arrived at the point where the jolly recreation of windsurfing becomes an athletic endeavour. It is a new style of sailing – not a battle of the biceps – which demands a new set of techniques, and a mental approach that complements the fast and furious spirit of high-wind sailing. Before examining the primary skills, the following key points, which recur in all manoeuvres and form the essence of funboard technique, should be highlighted:

1 Stance once again heads the rankings. Brute strength can compensate for poor light-wind posture, but strong winds expose the tiniest flaws. In a funboard context, a good stance guarantees comfort, enjoyment, long water sessions, early planing and good board speed.

2 Balance, you may think, is a natural ability, which you either have or have not. But in windsurfing it takes on many forms:

Static balance is the phenomenon that keeps tightrope walkers on their wires and lumberjacks on their logs. It is basically the art of remaining upright, with no support, on an unstable object such as a windsurfer at rest. It is certainly an asset but not essential to funboard sailing.

Rig balance When windsurfing, in light and strong winds, your arms and, when hooked in, your body are the contact points with the power source. The movements they make determine whether the rig de-powers, stalls or sets perfectly. On a funboard, balancing the rig is paramount, since

any loss of power can drop you straight off the plane.

Dynamic balance, the art of maintaining equilibrium when in motion, is the skill that makes for a good surfer, skier, skater, gymnast and funboard sailor. Most people will naturally lean inwards when going round a corner on a bicycle to counteract the centrifugal force. It is that ability to control the position of the body at speed through a loose knee and ankle action, while maintaining your spacial awareness, that makes for 'dynamic' performance.

3 Mastfoot pressure The power of the sail is transmitted into the board via two sources: your feet and the mastfoot. This power must be distributed between those two points in such a way that the board, despite fluctuations in the wind strength, remains at a constant angle in the water. Mastfoot pressure is also the means by which you manoeuvre the board into the beach and waterstarting positions and then lever yourself up.

4 Upright rig By holding the rig upright you expose all the sail area to the wind and therefore generate the maximum power for straight-line speed or lift in beach and waterstarts.

5 Timing is something of an abstract concept and one that is more com-

monly applied to ball games. But much can be learned from such a comparison. A cricket or tennis player who is timing his shots appears to achieve great power and accuracy with the minimum of effort. It is only when your timing is poor that windsurfing becomes a strength sport, for it is then that you are fighting the forces rather than letting them work for you. In gybing, for example, timing the rig change at the right moment when the board is travelling at its fastest and the rig is at its lightest makes for a sweet transition. In the waterstart, and equally in the most radical jumping and wave riding manoeuvres, you must aim to time your effort with the advent of a gust and have arms, legs, rig and other sources of power all working together for one explosive moment.

6 Mental attitude Go for it! No three words could sum up better the spirit needed to improve and master the most exciting manoeuvres. In strong winds, there is no time for hesitation and playing safe. Water is a soft medium, and shark attacks are rare, so hurl yourself at the ocean with reckless abandon. Remember, funboard sailing is a total immersion sport – dry hair is a sure sign that you have not been trying hard enough.

The funboard stance

'When the wind gets up, you have just got to lean out more,' declared one of the first manuals. A sensible, albeit rather vague, piece of advice. Leaning out in the old days meant throwing yourself back and taking the rig with you. Early publications displayed photos of daredevils with their backs skimming the waves and the sail cranked right over their heads to windward. "That's the way to get 'lift'," they said, "it makes the rig act like a wing."

Indeed it did act like a wing and directed the power upwards. However, despite the windsurfer's desire to be a creature of the air, his principle aim is to be driven along forwards. As for lift, the very act of the board going through the water creates lift – often too much in strong winds as sailors struggle to stop their boards bouncing out of control.

The strong-wind stance has undergone many changes over the past few years as sailors have experimented to find the best way of using body weight to control the rig and yet remain in a good position from which to footsteer the board. Not so long ago, they set their booms high for better leverage. Although it seemed comfortable when they were back in the straps and planing, during tacks and gybes the boom was in an unmanageable position above their heads.

The most damaging result of a high boom was that the only way of counteracting a strengthening wind was to lean the whole body and the rig out to windward, which was not only inefficient in that it reduced the effective sail area but also left you in a very vulnerable position, totally committed over the ocean. Moreover, only the upper body was being used to support the rig.

It was the massive American Fred Haywood who, in breaking the thirty-knot barrier in 1983, caused the world to stand up and take notice of his revolutionary sailing style. He set his boom low, wore a seat harness with a low hook and had long harness lines. When the wind blew he did not lean out, he merely sat down, and, in so doing, he kept the rig bolt upright and used every ounce of his fifteen stones to counterbalance the considerable force generated by a 6m² sail in thirty five knots of wind.

Everyone had been ignoring one grossly underrated, but wholly essential part of the anatomy – the bottom – and had been using their feeble forearms to take the strain. In most cases, the bottom is roughly your centre of gravity and the point of maximum ballast. By dropping it and lowering

your centre of gravity, you immediately become a more difficult object to knock over.

Taking the light to moderate wind stance (see Chapter 5) as your model, you can adapt it according to the following guidelines to get the most out of a funboard in planing conditions:
1 The head still looks forwards and to windward over the front shoulder with the shoulders themselves still parallel to the boom, facing the direction of travel.
2 Assuming you are not yet hooked in, the arms must now be extended. This diverts the strain away from the forearms and on to the stronger shoulder and back muscles and allows you to distance yourself from the sail, drop your weight to windward and still keep the rig upright.

In stronger winds, if you are not pulling equally on both arms, you will tire very quickly. It is crucial, therefore, that your hands are placed equidistant from the boom's balance point and, as before, no more than shoulder-width apart.

On large, long-boomed sails, where the draught of the sail is quite far back, your hands will be a long way down the boom. It is perhaps the commonest fault in funboard sailing to place the front hand too far forwards by the mast and to have the hands too widely spread. The effect on your technique will be devastating since you are unable to hold the rig away from you and keep the CE forwards. In water and beachstarts you cannot

All scrunched up! Bent arms, legs and arms too far apart, fighting the power – this sailor is still in first gear

The desired sitting position can be practised by placing a chair to windward of the board. There is extreme angulation at the waist. The bottom is dropped but the back remains upright and parallel with the mast. Note Stefan van den Berg's relaxed upper body position as he calls on the minimum of effort to support a 7.5m² sail

stop screwing up into the wind and likewise, when sailing off on a reach, you head straight into the wind as soon as you try to move back into the straps.

3 The hips and bottom are your most potent weapons with which to combat strong winds. As a beginner, you may, quite rightly, have been told not to stick your bottom out. But as an aspiring pro, that original sin is now permissible. However, the beginner uses his bottom as a last resort. Off balance forwards, on his toes, he shoots his bottom into the wind to try to level the balance, leaving himself bent double at the waist with his legs straight – an agonizing posture.

The correct method is to lower your bottom, *not* stick it out. As you bring on the power, sit down as if on a bar stool that is placed just to windward of the board. Like sitting normally, your legs are bent and your back is straight and upright, parallel with the mast. If the wind strengthens, you can straighten the legs, as if rocking backwards on the same bar stool, and angulate more at the waist. By so doing, you drop more ballast to windward but still keep the rig upright.

A further advantage of this technique is that you never have to sheet out. You can cope with gusts and lulls simply by swinging your bottom out and then pushing your hips forwards under the boom, while holding the rig perfectly still and upright. Remember that any movement you make with the sail, whether it be sheeting in or out, or pulling the rig to windward, disrupts the airflow, loses you power and slows you down.

4 In order to absorb the chop and stop the board skipping, the knees must remain soft. The feet, meanwhile, must be far back on the board over the planing area, and, except in extreme conditions, quite close together to make you more sensitive to the board's trim. If the wind allows, have your front foot in the rearmost of the front straps. Your back foot need only be placed in the back strap in rough conditions, otherwise leave it mobile on the centreline.

Trimming the board

Keeping the board level in both the lateral and longitudinal planes is the key to good board speed.

In the lateral plane it is the job of the feet to trim the board flat. If it is allowed to ride on its windward edge, the concaves stop creating lift and the board sticks to the water. With the back foot across the centreline, press down with the toes as you sheet in.

Some race boards arrive with offset back straps, which actually encourage you to put your back foot right on the windward edge. Such boards boast a domed deck which allows you to rest your heel against the 'hump' and push against the skeg. Since you are pushing across rather than down you can lift the windward rail with the heel and control the trim. It is a more advanced technique which is examined further in Chapter 12.

Keeping the board level in the longitudinal plane is a yet more subtle business. Some choose the direct method of putting their front foot right up by the mast and pressing hard to keep the nose down; and by so doing they force the front of the board into the water, increase the wetted area, cause excessive drag, stop the board planing freely and slow themselves right down.

So long as the wind does not drop altogether, you should be able to keep your feet in the straps and keep the board level by balancing the power of the rig between your feet and the mastfoot.

Watch out for visual signs of bad trim. If you look round to find other sailors surfing on your wake, it is a fair indication that you are sinking the tail. Lean forwards on to the rig, therefore, to take some of the weight off your feet and watch the back of the board rise up and accelerate. Conversely, if the nose is ploughing through the waves and you feel on the verge of a catapult, swing your body back over the tail. This situation is common only in strong winds.

Getting into the footstraps

As the board accelerates, the wetted area decreases and the CLR moves back, allowing the sail to be pulled down to close the slot. With the slot open (left), air can escape under the foot, reducing the pressure differential. When the slot is closed (right), the laminar flow is maintained

The familiar cry of people step-ping on to their first funboard is: "Why are the footstraps so far back? I can't get anywhere near them." Remember that they are designed to give you control of the board in strong winds, at which time you should be standing near the back of the board. Trying to get into them in light airs when the board is not planing is a vain and uncomfortable pursuit.

The key to the puzzle lies in good stance and mastfoot pressure. To avoid sinking the tail as you move back down the board, the rig must be held forwards with straight arms while your weight is taken on the rig and off your feet. Throughout the process, the board should show no visible signs of what is happening, remaining at a constant angle in the water.

What can appear baffling is the way

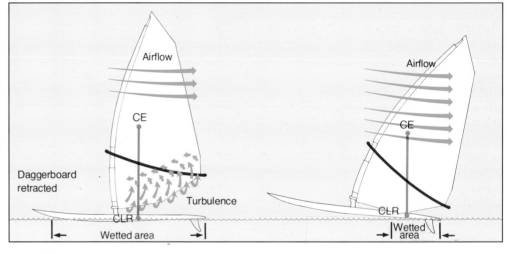

you end up with the weight of the sailor and the rig over the tail and yet not luff up. The explanation is simple. With the daggerboard retracted, the board's wetted surface decreases as it accelerates. Its CLR, therefore, moves further and further back until

in the most extreme conditions it will be the skeg itself. As you accelerate, therefore, you can draw the rig back slowly to close the slot between the foot of the sail and the deck and still keep the sail's CE over the board's pivot point.

1 Ready to accelerate. The feet are out of the straps as the board picks up speed. Note that the back foot is on the centreline between the front and back straps, in the perfect position to trim the board. Note also the position of the hands, in their proper place well down the boom.

2 As the board accelerates, straighten the arms to leave the rig upright with the CE forwards, sink down and take your weight on the boom so that you can move your front foot back into the forward of the two front straps, the back foot still in the same place.

3 As the board accelerates further and the wetted area decreases, you can move the front foot back into the rear front strap. See how the back foot keeps the board level despite all the movement down the board. Check the stance with the arms fully extended, the head looking forwards, the knees bent and the bottom lowered. Still a lot of weight is being taken on the rig.

Harness technique

Problems?

The majority of problems in this area are stance-related. The front hand is often the culprit. If it is too near the mast and the arms are spread wide and bent, you cannot hold the rig far enough forwards in the early stages and the board will make its way into the wind.

Insufficient mastfoot pressure and oversheeting will cause immediate luffing and are often the result of a closed stance with the shoulders turned into the sail.

Fear of being catapulted as they sheet in convinces people to anchor their back foot into the back strap before the board has a chance to move. Wrong! This actually increases the risk of being thrown since the back foot will sink the tail, cause drag, stop the board accelerating and so increase the apparent wind in the sail.

4 As the board reaches full speed and starts to plane just on the tail, draw the rig right back to close the slot. Only move the back foot into a strap if you feel insecure.

Gruesome tales of yore still make some people eye the harness with mistrust. Visions of themselves face down in the water, tied inextricably to the boom following a high-flying, twisting catapult fall persuade them to label the harness as a strictly 'experts only' luxury.

Such horror stories are now folk-lore. The introduction of no-tangle hooks and quick-release systems has made it safe to start using a harness as soon as you are sailing comfortably in a force 3 to 4. In fact, without one you will be exhausted long before you have had a chance to master the funboard manoeuvres, unless you happen to wear your underpants on the outside of your tights!

The early high hook waistcoat style of harness saved energy but slowed you down. Racers used them only in an emergency. When hooked in, they found themselves too close to the rig, they felt cramped, less mobile and less sensitive to changes in wind strength and direction. The racer who was the last to resort to the harness in strong winds often came out on top.

Today the situation has been totally reversed. Seat and waist harnesses not only save energy but actually improve performance. With their low hooks and bottom support, they place you in a better stance, allow you to make more efficient use of your body weight, hold a bigger sail and therefore go faster – so long as you are using the right technique.

Setting up the lines

Correctly set-up harness lines automatically improve your stance, whereas lines that are ill-placed or

Bjorn Dunkerbeck hooked into a slalom race. The long lines allow for straight arms and an upright rig

the wrong length totally pervert it.

The theory is simple. The apex of the loop should correspond to the balance point of the boom; so that when hooked in, your centre of gravity is pulling directly against the CE of the sail, leaving your arms free to make the fine adjustments.

If your technique is sound, you should look the same sailor in and out of the harness, a feat which is only possible if your lines are deep enough to allow you to drop your bottom and sail with straight arms.

Setting up the lines is a crucial part of preparation. Check them each time before going out, remembering that

Harness technique

1 With the lines loosely attached, hang against the sail on the beach in your normal stance (find a sheltered nook if it is very windy), and move your hands closer and closer together until you can support it with one hand. This represents the balance point of the boom.

2 Make a mental note of it and then slide the line into place so that the straps are equidistant from the balance point just inside shoulder-width apart.

3 To hook in and check their position, pull the rig towards you by bending the arms slightly, push the hips forwards ...

4 ... let the line come up under the hook ...

5 ... before extending the arms again and taking the weight of the rig on your body, all the time keeping your weight committed to windward. Note the length of line, it is deep enough to allow you to sail with the arms just slightly bent.

6 If the lines are in the right place your arms should be equally loaded. The final test is to let go with one or both hands for a couple of seconds without the rig twisting away.

their position on the boom will be different for each of your sails.

Unfortunately, this is not the end of the story. On the water there is more wind passing over the sail due to the board moving through the air, which even on the most stable sails causes the CE to move back a little. Either predict this by moving the line further back than is comfortable on the beach, or go out with the ends just loosely attached so that you can adjust the line easily when on the water. Once you are comfortable, come back to shore in and tighten them up.

Remember the simple adjustment rule: if the front arm feels overloaded, move both ends of the line forwards; if the back arm is having to do more work, move both ends of the line back.

7 To unhook simply pull the rig sharply towards you; the tension will come off the line and it will drop out of the hook.
8 Error! *Do not* hook in by moving your body to the sail. If the rig drops to leeward, you will be pulled on to your toes and then your face with no chance of hooking out.

Water practice
Your first session on the water should be in about a force 3; something to lean against but not enough to keep launching you into space.

Initially, just practise hooking in and out to familiarize yourself with the position of the hook relative to the line. *Do not* cheat by grabbing the line with your hand. Trying such a stunt in a strong wind could be tragic. Your aim is to hook in and out without taking your eyes off the road ahead. The biggest wave of the day invariably arrives when your eyes are gazing at the harness hook!

Refining the stance
Learning to relax is perhaps the biggest hurdle to overcome. Ironically, some people grip so hard with their

hands during the first sessions that they use more energy hooked in than they do hooked out.

Revert back to your normal stance. With a low hook, low boom and longer lines, you sit down in order to bring tension on the line. Therein lies the key; sitting, *not* leaning out and throwing the shoulders back. Remember that bar stool.

Now that you are suspended by your bottom, you are in a position to take all the weight on the rig. You act like a pendulum, swinging in and out, forwards and backwards by bending and straightening the legs.

Coping with gusts is the idle man's dream. The athletic way of resisting a lull might be to unhook, leap out of the footstraps and run forwards on the board – it is also the most inefficient. By running forwards you stamp the whole length of the board into the water, disrupt the sail, open the slot and bring the board to a halt.

Far better and less tiring is to leave your feet in the straps, remain hooked in and, as you sail into the lull, simply bend the legs and swing forwards towards the mast. By so doing you immediately take the weight off your feet and transfer it, via the harness line, on to the boom and through the mastfoot. The tail does not sink, the board maintains the same trim angle, the sail does not move, the laminar flow continues uninterrupted, the slot stays closed and you keep planing. Only if the lull is severe and prolonged must you unhook and step forwards on the board.

As a gust hits, your first reaction must be to sit down lower for stability, before straightening your legs to

Harness technique

take your centre of gravity further back and more outboard. You now have more of the power going through your feet in order to control the tail of the board and keep in contact with the water.

It is easy to overemphasize the lazy aspect of harness technique, so before you become an armchair athlete, take heed of the following:

1 *Do not* hook in until you are in a comfortable stance and are planing.

2 *Do not* hook in when jumping a wave, riding a wave or when gybing.

3 *Do not* hook in if grossly overpowered, unless it is the only means to get back to the beach.

The vast majority of people sail with harness lines that are too short, leaving them dangerously close to the rig with no room to manoeuvre. Longer lines get you away from the sail, allow you to keep the rig upright and make you a hard object to pull over.

When it all goes wrong . . .

The time will come, as it comes to all, when, despite all precautions, you will be asked to perform that most spectacular of involuntary dismounts, the hooked-in catapult.

In moderate winds it is really quite a pleasant experience, for once the sail has fallen past the vertical, it backwinds and you will float gracefully down on top of the sail. Just keep your arms straight and your head up. After splashdown, release the line with a sweep of the hand.

In strong winds you have little control over your destiny, so just relax and enjoy the ride!

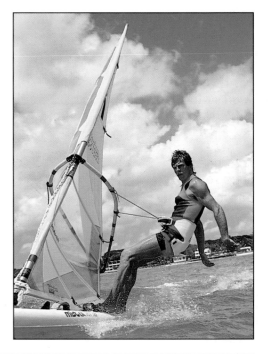

The hooked-in catapult is one of the most exciting manoeuvres! If you feel yourself going, relax, keep your head up and away from the boom and try to avoid twisting

The beachstart

For a long time, the beachstart has been grouped under the general heading of 'Advanced Funboard Manoeuvres' and has carried the warning label: 'Beware! Difficult. Good sailors and strong winds only!'

In truth, it can and should be learned at a very early stage, in winds of force 2 upwards, as soon as you have basic rig control. You will not need reminding how uphauling in the shorebreak is an exercise that can leave you broken-masted, as well as physically and mentally drained. The beachstart is a skill that immediately transforms your career by making launching into waves a pleasure rather than a lottery.

There are two types of well-practised beachstart. One where you dig the skeg into the sand, step on board and wait for the tide or the next wave to float you, whichever is the sooner; and the other where you control the power in the sail and use it to lift you into your normal sailing position. Obviously, the latter method is preferable, not only because your skeg remains intact, but also because it comprises the essence of the waterstart.

Lining up the board

It is not possible to beachstart unless the board is lined up correctly, an exercise which once again is achieved with minimum muscle power just by harnessing the wind.

Remember, your daggerboard must be retracted. The board will now pivot about the skeg. If you imagine that the tail of the board has been nailed to the spot, you can see how by lifting up or pushing down on the rig you can apply pressure to the mastfoot and make the board head up or bear away. It is as if the board were

1 With the dagger retracted, place yourself upwind of the board, keep the sail full and control the power.

2 Now lift up with the front hand and the nose will swing upwind towards you.

3 As the nose passes to the inside of you through the wind, gybe the sail by releasing the back hand.

4 Place your old back hand on the mast and the old front hand on the boom. Bear the board away . . .

5 . . . applying mastfoot pressure by pushing down with the front hand. Walk to the back of the board . . .

6 . . . transfer your front hand to the boom and, with the board across the wind, you are ready to beachstart.

The beachstart

spinning around that nail.

This is an indispensable funboard skill since it allows you to point the board in any direction without having to manhandle it. Should you happen to fall inshore amongst the white water, you can quickly stand up, grab hold of the mast, turn the board through 180 degrees and beachstart away, before the next wave has a chance to spit you ashore.

You can learn the principles of mastfoot steering by removing your skeg and experimenting with the push-pull movement of the rig on the beach, before refitting the skeg and spending some time in shallow water just spinning the board around upwind and downwind.

The procedure
You beachstart by stepping up on to the back of the board, from where you let the power in the rig pull you forwards into your normal stance.

It is as easy as it sounds so long as you abide by the fundamental rules:
1 Give in to the power that is pulling you forwards, *do not* fight against it. The board, like a racehorse straining at the bit, wants to go forwards. Do not rein it in but give it its head.
2 Control the wind. This is the secret of success in the beachstart and the waterstart. In both cases, there are two ways of losing and creating power:
a. Sheeting in and out as perfected in lesson one.
b. Moving the rig in the leeward/windward plane. By pulling the rig over your head to windward, you decrease the sail area exposed to the wind and reduce the power. By straightening the arms up and exposing more of the sail to the wind, you increase the power and the lift.

3 Get the rig upright. Once it is upright you can pull yourself up under the boom without bringing the rig down over your head.
4 Timing. The beachstart is effortless if you time your movement on to the board and the straightening of the arms with a gust.

Practice
The ideal conditions for practising the beachstart are a waveless, shallow shelving beach, a long board (330cm plus) and a force 3–4 blowing side or side onshore.

You can save time and energy by trying the beachstart first on dry land, practising stepping on to the board in the right place, straightening the arms and controlling the power. Remember to retract the daggerboard and locate the mast-track in the middle or just behind.

1 Carry the board into thigh-deep water, deep enough to prevent the skeg grounding. For more positive control of the rig at this stage, keep the front hand on the mast above the boom and the back hand on the boom. Hold the rig over to windward and stop the board from luffing by maintaining pressure on the mastfoot.

2 Place the front hand on the boom in its normal place and bear the board away by leaning down on the rig so that it lies just downwind of a beam reach while walking towards the back of the board (the footstrap area). See how the rig is kept low to expose less sail area to the wind.

3 Place the back foot on the centreline in between the front and back straps, controlling the position of the board by pushing down and pulling up on the rig.

The beachstart is similar to stepping up on to a bench. You must lean forwards until your centre of gravity is over your bent knee, before trying to stand up. Straightening the leg too early will mean you flop back into the water and is the commonest mistake in this and the waterstart

Problems?

The vast majority of problems, as usual, can be traced back to a poor stance, so before you get desperate with frustration, check your posture and especially the positions of the front hand and the shoulders.

The approach "I can't get my feet anywhere near the board," is a common cry, and, while it may be the result of a boom set far too high, it is more likely caused by approaching the board from the mastfoot area. Remember to walk in from the rear windward quarter, so that you are standing by the footstraps.

Sideshore currents aggravate the problem as they catch the fin and sweep the back of the board away from you. The only solution is to keep walking downwind while bearing the nose away through mastfoot pressure until you are next to the board. If you

get the back foot on early, you can use it to control the back of the board.

Heading up into the wind is probably the commonest way of fluffing the beachstart and may be due to either of the following:

1 Stamping on the tail. This will make the board spin round like a top on the skeg. Walk in from the windward side, not from straight behind,

and place the back foot further forwards.

2 Oversheeting. If you oversheet with the back hand, you will stall the sail, no power will go through the mastfoot to keep the board level, the tail will sink and the board will luff. Make sure your shoulders are open and facing the direction of travel and *do not* try to pull yourself up with the back hand.

Falling back to windward indicates that you have tried to stand up before your centre of gravity is over the centreline. The movement is exactly the same as stepping up on to a bench. You lift your leg, rock forwards over your bent knee and then straighten it. Then aim to get forwards on the board.

The flop to windward also indicates that the sailor has attempted to heave himself up on to the board by pulling on the boom before the rig was upright.

Getting overpowered and falling in to leeward reveals a lack of anticipation and poor rig control. Sheeting out is the emergency measure of preventing the plunge. It is far better, however, to keep the power on as you rise up and control it by bending the

4 Preferably on the arrival of a gust of wind, straighten the arms vigorously to get the rig upright, swing forwards on the front arm towards the mastfoot, rock up over your bent back leg, staying as compact as possible . . .

5 . . . before levering yourself up under the boom. As you rise up, place the front foot in front of the straps initially to level the board out and promote planing. With the rig so upright, you must stay low to withstand the surge of power.

The beachstart

Setting off in waves is a question of timing. Hold your board and rig clear of the white water, wait for a wave to wash through and then launch in the deep water behind it. At all costs, stand on the ocean side of your board

knees and holding the rig slightly over to windward. Remember that as you accelerate, the apparent wind moves forwards and the force in the sail lessens, allowing you to slip quickly into your proper stance with the rig upright.

Strong winds and waves
In strong winds, the rules change slightly: getting on is not so much the problem as staying on. Your aim, therefore, must be to step straight into the footstraps so that you are secure and ready to meet the first oncoming wave.

You must keep the rig very low before stepping on, time your effort between waves and be sailing the board from the moment your feet leave the ocean floor.

Waves represent quite a challenge

during the launch phase. Good timing and a modicum of aggression are necessary if you are to conquer the foam.

On the beach, study the break be-

fore selecting a launch site, away from breakwaters and other obstacles, where the waves are breaking with least venom. Time your launch so that you drop the board on top of a breaking wave and try to make your getaway before it has receded.

In relentless, tightly-spaced waves, you will probably have to survive at least one barrage of white water. For better grip, hold the mast with both hands, then, as the wave approaches, shove the board over the white water, remembering the following essential safety points:

1 To avoid receiving a mouthful of fibreglass, always stand upwind and up-wave of the board.
2 Be sure to hold the rig well over to windward. If the clew catches the wave, the rig will be ripped out of your hands. A rig lying unattended in breaking waves is in mortal peril.

If you get caught in the shorebreak, grab the mast with both hands and thrust the board through the wave

The beach recovery

In gentle sea conditions, landing is simply a beachstart in reverse. You come out of the straps as you approach the beach, sheet out to control your speed, step off (back foot first) as you enter the shallows before the skeg grounds and then, holding the rig over to windward, either push the board up the beach on its rail, or, if possible, lift the whole lot clear and lay it safely on the shore.

In waves, however, there are other points to consider:

1 If the waves are dumping, you risk being caught and flung mercilessly on the shingle.

2 The depth of the water is ever-changing. It is easy to run aground and damage the skeg or skeg box.

3 The surf possesses uncanny power. Unless you quickly get the board and rig out of the water, the retreating waves can 'suck' them back into the rinse cycle. The end of the story is all too familiar.

Landing safely in even the wildest seas is merely a case of keeping an eye on your surroundings. Obviously you do not want to time your run home on the 'wave of the day'. As you approach the beach, therefore, keep looking behind you to spot potential dangers and regulate your speed so that you are sailing between waves. You want to sail to the beach not be washed up it.

The water is perilously shallow in front of waves, so as the shore approaches sail in on the back of a wave in order to make your landing safe, both for you and your board.

1 Sail in on the back of a wave and take your feet out of the straps before you reach the break zone.

2 Step off in thigh-deep water and immediately take hold of the board using your preferred carrying technique.

3 Keep it well clear of the surf and hurry ashore before the next wave knocks you off balance.

4 Cartwheeling boards and rigs are a liability, so take time to lay them on the beach in such a way that you present the smallest possible area to the wind – that is, with the mast tip pointing downwind, the mast itself parallel to the wind direction and the board on top, still attached to the rig with its nose pointing into the wind.

In all but the wildest conditions, the board and rig are thus safe so long as you plan to return within a few minutes. Otherwise, find a sheltered spot out of the wind and direct sunlight.

The waterstart

Having started life as nothing more than a freestyle trick where the sailor lowered his bottom into the water before letting the wind pull him back on to the board, the waterstart has become an indispensable weapon in the funboarder's armoury. It is the safest, least tiring method of getting going in strong winds and the only way of setting sinkers in motion.

Its advantages are plain to see. Unlike uphauling where, stationary aboard an unstable platform, you have to pull the sail up against the wind, in the waterstart you use the power of the wind to pull you up so that you arrive on board in your sailing position already moving.

Despite its apparent simplicity, the mystery of the waterstart prevails. However, there is no real mystery. The problem is that it is easy to get disorientated and forget where the wind is coming from when up to your neck in a foreign element. Reason can soon yield to anger and frustration; and, if this happens, you are doomed, for the waterstart is a thinking person's manoeuvre.

The waterstart can be broken down into two parts: the rig recovery (freeing the sail from the water) and the act of being pulled on board. The former demands much the same technique as picking a sail up off the beach while the latter is little more than a deep-water beachstart.

The rig recovery
Flying the rig has inspired some extraordinary feats of athleticism. There are those who, as at last-ditch attempt to release the sail, have swum to the sea bed, pushed off with arms outstretched, aiming to hit it with the force of a leaping salmon and punch it clear.

It is not, however, a task for the scuba diver and you should be able to recover the rig quite easily. It is merely a case of swimming the rig into a position where the mast lies across the wind upwind of the clew. As you lift the mast, the wind can blow under the rig's longest and most stable edge and lift the sail.

You use the wind to free the rig and the rig to manoeuvre the board into

Breathing is an important part of rig recovery, so keep your head above water and delegate all the hard work to the wind

position. Once you have it in your mind that the wind will do the work, the battle is half won.

Problems?
If the end of the boom catches as you try to release the rig (often a problem with big sails), grab the mast with both hands and pull down with all your might. If you relinquish the battle, the rig will flip over forcing you to start all over again. If this happens continually, you may be guilty of pushing the mast straight up, whereas it is the motion into the wind that frees the clew. In strong winds, keep the mast close to the water.

If the sail backwinds you have probably let yourself drift downwind. Keep the legs pumping to maintain

your position upwind of the board, and pull down with the back hand to fill the sail from the right side.

Short cuts

In heavy seas and shark-infested waters, you want to spend as little time in the water as possible. Once you have mastered the basic recovery technique, you can experiment with ways to cut corners.

1 If the clew is lying upwind of the mast, rather than swim the mast through 180 degrees, grab hold of the end of the boom, lift it and let the wind flip the rig over. The mast will then be lying across the wind.

2 If the rig is lying downwind of the board, with the board itself lying roughly across the wind, take hold of the mast and swim the rig towards the back of the board. Then, holding the back footstrap with the back hand and the mast with the front hand, drag the rig across the back of the board. The boom passing over the solid base of the tail lifts the rig up and out.

3 If the rig has fallen to windward, with the tip of the mast pointing directly into the wind, hold the front of the board and swim it into the wind. This draws the mast across the wind from where you can continue as normal.

Getting up

The only difference between the beachstart and the last part of the waterstart is that in the latter you cannot spring off the sea bed, but have to rely entirely on wind power to lift you on to the board.

In winds below force 5, it is not sufficient to lie in the water and expect to

1 Grab the mast about 1m/3ft above the boom and swim it upwind, lifting it gently to shake off the water. It will soon start to feel light.

3 That should force enough wind under the sail to free the end of the boom.

2 When it is lying roughly across the wind, using an aggressive arm movement, pull the rig up and into the wind.

4 Take control of the rig immediately by sheeting in and placing the front hand on the boom in its normal place. Continue to swim upwind and towards the mastfoot, keeping constant pressure on the rig to bear the board away. With the board lying just off the wind, you are in perfect shape to waterstart.

The waterstart

be hoisted aloft. To be successful you must get the most from the sail by pushing it upright and limit your arc of movement by making yourself a small and compact bundle.

It is important to understand your itinerary on to the board. You roll up over a bent back leg, *forwards* along the board, and then pull yourself up *under* the boom.

As with the beachstart, once your centre of gravity is over the centreline and the rig is upright, the job is done. From that position you can lever yourself up and forwards by pulling down on the mastfoot with the front hand.

As with all these skills, nothing is possible unless you are in the correct stance. Even when floating with the rig in the water, the head must be looking forwards and to windward to spot the gusts; your shoulders must be parallel to the boom; your arms must be straight and your hands must be down the boom, equidistant from the balance point, no more than shoulder-width apart. Should your hands be too far apart or too close to the boom, you will not be able to hold the rig far enough forwards to prevent the board luffing, nor upright enough to get the essential lift.

Before practising the manoeuvre, run through the following check list:

1 Make sure the boom is shoulder height or lower. Any higher and you will have trouble getting your feet near the board.

2 Locate the track at or near the back to help you get the rig more upright.

3 The daggerboard, if fitted, must be retracted.

4 A force 4–5 is ideal for learning.

The key points of the waterstart are: stance, rig control and timing. If you work on these three, success is not far away. Have a clear picture of what you are trying to achieve and beware of the following common errors:

Feet in the straps Only in very strong winds when you want to arrive on board in your securest position do you put your feet in the straps before you rise up. To do so in moderate winds will prevent you from thrusting the rig upright and will cause you to drift downwind, thereby losing power.

Luffing up is the most common symptom of failure to keep pressure on the mastfoot. A secondary cause might be faulty back foot placement. Some people try to place it flat on the board when in the water. For want of rubber ankles, this is impossible and they compromise by twisting it forwards, thereby making it impossible to rock up over the knee while unbalancing the whole lower body. During the struggle, the board invariably heads up. Remember, just rest the heel on the windward edge.

Front or back foot first?

There are some good sailors who place their strongest leg on the board first. On one tack this will be the front foot. Although logically more awkward, since it requires you to shuffle forwards on the board as you rise up, it is worth trying if you are having trouble getting up on one tack.

Practice

Ironically, the worst place to practise the waterstart is in the water. It is the most effortless manoeuvre when you

1 With the board facing just off a beam reach, swim in towards the back windward half of the board and place your back heel on the windward rail in between the front and back straps. Keep pressure on the mastfoot to stop the board heading up and tread water with the front foot for stability and to keep you high in the water.

2 Having decided to go (preferably with a gust), throw the rig upright and forwards by fully extending the arms and explode from the water like a coiled spring.

3 Having got as close to the board as possible, rock up over the bent back leg so that the back foot now straddles the centreline. See how the upper body swings forwards under the boom and bears down on the mastfoot to keep the board level.

4 The front leg remains in the water until the final moment. It acts like a daggerboard and stops you drifting sideways and, if kicked hard enough, provides both stability and extra lift. As you pull yourself up under the boom, place the front foot in front of the straps until the board has picked up speed.

The waterstart

With his hands so far apart, this sailor will be unable to apply mastfoot pressure to stop the board luffing. With bent arms and a low rig he will need a hurricane to lift him

can do it, and the most exhausting when you cannot. Prepare yourself for the water with some dry-land and light-wind practice.

Familiarize yourself with the rig recovery by laying the board and rig in the shallows in various positions. Then decide which way you would swim it. To make it more realistic, wade out into waist-deep water, so that you can practise swimming and the arm movement to free the rig. Being on terra firma will save untold energy early on.

Likewise, you do not have to be out

With straight legs you are a heavy package; but by bending the knees and bringing your bottom right up to the edge of the board, you shorten your arc of movement and require a meagre force to haul you up

of your depth to practise the waterstart itself. On a shallow shelving beach, perform deeper and deeper beachstarts until you can no longer spring up using your feet.

On dry land, try lying down with the sail on top of you, and then, by bending the knees, straightening the arms and thrusting with the hips and bottom, try to stand up.

On a long board in light airs, lie down full length on the board and control the direction through mastfoot pressure. Then stand up again by levering yourself up under the boom using the front arm. Alternatively, try sailing along dragging the front leg in the water; the action of getting up again is exactly the same as the last part of the waterstart.

Equipment

Ultimately, you can waterstart with any type of board or rig. When learn-ing, however, it is wise to use a funboard that you can uphaul with ease should you experience teething problems.

Sails pose more of a dilemma. Take note of the following:
1 The shorter the boom, the easier it is to fly the rig. Sails much bigger than 6m^2 are something of a struggle.
2 Fully-battened RAF sails create a lot of power, generally fit short booms and are good for learning with. In the water, however, the camber can cradle a trough of water. Before flying the rig, rotate the battens so that the fullness faces up.
3 Camber induced sails are a positive liability to the first-time waterstarter. They generate plenty of power but the widened luff tube holds gallons of water. If the rig has had time to sink, you are facing a lost cause.
4 Soft sails are light and easy to manoeuvre in the water and have no vices.

The carve gybe

No one manoeuvre captures the quintessence of funboard sailing quite like the carve gybe. Within that short five-second period all those essential elements of stance, commitment, timing and mobility have to gel to produce a fluid, dynamic and yet effortless manoeuvre. But while the visually more spectacular stunts such as loops, barrel rolls, donkey kicks and so on require a special and rare set of conditions, the carve gybe can be performed on a placid lake or a heaving ocean in as little as eleven knots of wind.

Far from being a 'difficult' manoeuvre, the carve gybe can be attempted just as soon as you are sailing confidently in the footstraps. It remains, however, a constant challenge. Every gybe is different on account of the infinite number of variables that confront you on the water. Board length, rocker line, sail size, wind strength, sea state, your own weight, your speed and the radius of the turn all affect your timing and your body positions and how you distribute your weight. It is not surprising, therefore, that even the world's top funboarders are constantly honing their gybing skills in the endless search for perfection.

The greatest influence on your technique will be the type of funboard you are using. A long board (330cm plus) displays more sedentary gybing characteristics and cannot be cranked over to the same extremes as a 260cm wave board.

However hard you kick a donkey, it will not win the Derby; on the other hand, you stand a good chance of finishing the race without falling off.

For learning purposes, therefore, the longer board is preferable since it is both predictable and forgiving (although having progressed to a sinker you might change those adjectives to 'boring' and 'unresponsive'). It is also safer. The complete sailor, however, should be able to adapt his technique to deal with both.

The basic body positions are the same for gybing long and short boards, although the timing of the rig and foot change and your foot placement vary according to the speed of the turn. The long board, for instance, due to its size, long rails and straight rocker line, is reluctant to carve all the way through the wind without help from the rig. It is wise, therefore, to come out of the turn clew first and change the feet before flipping the sail. When learning, this allows you to balance yourself during the final wobbly stages. The same technique is also used on short boards, especially when using big sails. There is, however, a more fluid technique which is examined in Chapter 9.

So much happens in such a short space of time in the carve gybe that it is essential to have a clear image of the finished article in your mind before breaking it down and isolating the various stages.

Footsteering the board up and downwind is the best way to practise the carving action. With the front foot in the rear front strap and the back foot unanchored, plane off on a beam reach. Staying sheeted in, lean on the downwind rail and then on the upwind rail, noting how the board reacts. On every reach, lean harder on the edges, bending your knees more and applying more pressure to the back foot. Make a mental note of how much of the rail you can engage before the board 'sticks'. Most long boards only turn on the back third, the area behind the footstraps.

Run through the following check list before your practice session:

1 You must have planing wind, force 4 minimum, allowing you to sail comfortably in the straps.

2 Select the right size sail – one that drives you effortlessly on to the plane and allows you to settle into a comfortable, relaxed stance, sheeted in with the slot closed, and the feet in the back straps. It is reasonable to assume that, if you enter the gybe cramped and uncomfortable, you will come out the other end in a similar state, if indeed you come out at all.

3 Your mastfoot must be located at or near the back of the track to minimize the planing area. Your daggerboard, of course, must be retracted.

4 Have you found a flat water location? Chop is the carve gyber's nightmare. It grabs at the rails, makes the board bounce through the turns and causes spin-out.

5 Faced by the open ocean, you can delay the gybe for hours in search of the perfect moment. Marker buoys not only give you a target but also provide you with a point of reference throughout the turn to help you time the rig change.

The carve gybe

1 On a beam reach, bear the board away a little and let the rig pull you into a more upright stance over the centreline of the board. You should now be on your fastest point of sailing. Prepare for the gybe by unhooking and checking the water behind and to leeward for solid objects. If the back foot is in a strap, take it out and place it on the leeward (inside) rail, approximately eighteen inches behind the front foot, facing forwards and in.

2 The carve is initiated by driving the knees towards the centre of the turning circle and by committing all your weight to the back foot in order to engage the leeward rail. Note that the arms are straight and the rig, like the knees and body, is leaning into the turn.

3 The body holds the position. The back foot keeps constant pressure on the rail. There is angulation at the hips so that while the knees are driving forwards and in, the upper body remains relatively upright and parallel to the mast. The head is still and looking forwards, *not* at the feet.

5 As soon as the sailor arrives in the clew first position on the new broad reach, the feet are changed. The old front foot pivots out of its strap on to the centreline, while the new front foot is placed in front of the straps to level the board out.

6 The rig flip follows immediately. The back hand releases the boom and grabs the mast just below the boom connection, de-powers the sail and grabs the mast . . .

7 . . . it then pulls the rig across the body to windward so that the new back hand can reach down the boom without the sailor having to bend forwards at the waist.

A relaxed yet dynamic posture makes Anders Bringdal look unshakeable as he gybes around the mark of a course race. Although he is sinking the tail to prevent the long rails grabbing, his weight is committed forwards. He is sheeting in hard and holds the rig upright for maximum drive through the turn

4 The board reaches the critical downwind stage, but continues to carve round thanks to continued pressure on the inside rail. See how the sailor's centre of gravity is totally committed to the inside of the turn and how control is maintained through bent knees.

8 As the sailor falls back against the sail to sheet in, the front hand takes hold of the boom in its normal place. Only once the board starts to plane again does he move back into the straps.

The rig change

The sequence of hand movements in the rig change is exactly the same as that for the flare gybe. The rig itself, however, plays an entirely different role. In the flare gybe, it is scooped to windward to turn the board, but in the carve gybe the rig is leaned in to leeward, where it provides the forward thrust to drive the board around a depressed inside edge.

In light winds, it does no harm to sail along doing sail 180° after sail 180° so that the hand movements become crisp, positive and automatic.

Speed and commitment

It is hard to practise a state of mind. Nevertheless, before a gybing session you must give yourself a stiff talking to and make it quite clear that disappointment is guaranteed if you decide to play safe. With so much to think about and so little time in which to act, it is tempting to sheet out on the approach in order to slow down and score a couple of extra seconds. This is disastrous for a number of reasons. For example, the board needs as much speed and momentum as possible to carry it smoothly through the gybe. Similarly, as you sheet out, you cut off the power to the mastfoot. The board, therefore, sinks a little, the planing area increases and you have every chance of stalling.

The carve gybe

Problem areas

The approach to the gybe is where all the trouble starts. Lack of speed, as already mentioned, is catastrophic, as is poor weight distribution. It is a common fault to see people still leaning out to windward as they start carving. As the board begins to accelerate through the turn, they simply get left behind. At best the board levels out downwind, at worst they are flung to the outside.

It is essential to have your weight over the board before you initiate the turn. Your hips bring the rest of the body forwards and inboard to anticipate the centrifugal force.

The arms Many people bend the arms and pull the rig down over their heads as they start the turn, for fear of getting overpowered by the rig as they bear away. As a result, they kill the power and, with the weight of the sailor and the rig over the back of the board, the tail sinks, the board slows down, stops carving and the manoeuvre has a premature end.

You must keep the arms straight and hold the rig upright and well out in front of you for maximum power. Moreover, if you maintain a comfortable distance between yourself and the boom, you will not get tied up in the rig change.

The carving action Straight, stiff legs are a drastic but curable windsurfing malaise. Very similar to snow skiing, it is the knees that do most of the work in the carve gybe. If they are locked out, your centre of gravity is too high and you are forced to bend forwards at the waist which impairs your dynamic balance and board control.

However, uttering simply "bend the knees", like an overworked ski instructor, can mislead people into squatting down into that old Turkish toilet stance. A more apt instruction is: "push the knees forwards". They work as one unit and anticipate the board's course by driving in almost to the extent of touching the water to leeward. At the same time, they must remain supple to iron out the bumps

By sheeting out too soon and transferring his weight to his front foot, this sailor has buried the whole length of the inside rail. This gybe will finish before the last act

and keep the board in contact with the water.

Remember that a long board will only carve around on the back third. The back foot, therefore, plays a vital role in applying enough pressure to the inside rail to keep the front two-thirds out of the water. At the same

1 As a result of bent arms and a straight body position the board falls quickly off the plane.

2 This leaves the sailor cramped and overpowered in the clew first position.

3 When he releases the back hand, the rig falls behind and to leeward, sending the board spinning into the wind.

time it must not stamp on the back and sink the tail, but must apply subtle and constant pressure in order to hold the board at the same angle all the way round and keep up the speed.

The rig change is another area where people play safe, electing to shuffle their hands down the boom and not sheet in until they have anchored themselves in the straps. Such a policy is counter-productive since the longer the sail remains de-powered, the greater the chance of the board heading up. Moreover, the more you allow the board to slow down, the greater the force in the sail and the harder it becomes to control.

Modern sails, with their fullness locked near the mast, are hard to hold clew first, so flip the rig as soon as the board passes through the wind and you feel pressure on the back arm.

The rig change is so much easier if you keep the rig upright and at arm's length in front of you. If you scoop it, you will find it behind you and hanging down to leeward as you come out of the turn. Before you have time to haul it forwards and back to the balance point, the board squirts into the wind.

The board is far more stable when on the move, so bring the power back on as soon as you can and keep up your speed!

Stefan van den Berg performing a boom to boom rig change

Chapter 9 **SHORT BOARD SAILING**

Words are hopelessly inadequate to describe the thrill that you will experience during your first reach on a short board. After a couple of doses, short board fever can become a violent addiction. However, some will never make the step from long to short, either because they are convinced that they are not good enough or because they attempt it too soon. You do not have to live on the beach to learn to sail a short board, but you must have considerable strong-wind experience and be able to waterstart. Short boards are full of surprises, both good and bad, so approach with caution.

First steps

Perhaps the most concise description of 'the short board experience' is that it is like sailing just the back half of a long board. There is no 'dead wood'. Everything beneath you is wired up and alive and if you touch something, it goes off.

It may sound simplistic to say that the short board has less volume and has a nasty habit of sinking, but therein lies the crux of the matter. Long boards absorb minor miscalculations like a sponge. You can clunk around their ample decks in a crisis and although they might wobble with discontent, you usually escape with a warning. On short boards, however, there is no padding. If you make an error, you are swiftly punished.

Trim and stance
The short board's sensitivity makes it the ultimate test of trim and stance. It obeys instructions instantly – a truly positive trait so long as the instructions are intended – but since a turn can be initiated by the tweak of a toe or the flexing of a buttock, any foot movements have to be light and positive and kept to a minimum. It is so easy to upset the trim of a short board and stop it planing that you must endeavour to keep your feet in the same

place and compensate for the vagaries of the wind and sea by subtle movement of the knees, ankles, hips and bottom.

Sensitivity and mobility of the lower body must be complemented by equally sensitive rig and power control. To keep the board planing, the trim angle of the sail must be constant and the forces shared between feet and mastfoot in such a way as to keep the board at its most efficient angle in the water.

Potential problem areas
1 Oversheeting, as a result of poor stance or poor balance, disrupts the laminar flow, kills the power and causes the board to sink and head up.
2 Sheeting out, through lack of anticipation and failure to use hips, knees and bottom to compensate for gusts, means the board jumps on and off the plane.
3 Overloading the mastfoot buries the nose.
4 Sitting on the back foot stops the tail releasing and causes luffing.

Such accurate harnessing of the forces requires great concentration. It is perhaps that as much as the technical skill which confounds the first-time short boarder. There is no time to

'cruise' or scratch your nose, for if you stop, you sink. The consistently intense level at which you are asked to perform places a hitherto unknown strain on your energy reserves and, given that during the initial forays you will be tense and prone to overcompensating, total exhaustion can be minutes away. Your choice, therefore, of location, equipment and conditions is essential for safe, quick progress.

Location
Although you may have a wave board, waves are the last things you want on your first outings. Great fun later on, they simply add one more variable to the equation.

Traditionally, short boards evoke images of stranded sailors drifting helplessly out to sea, deserted by the wind, unable to waterstart. To allow you to concentrate on the task in hand rather than the business of staying alive, you must select a totally safe location. The ideal would be an enclosed, shallow bay, sheltered from the waves but not the wind. You will have to get used to the idea of water-starting every time, but being able to walk back to base in a crisis helps the confidence enormously.

Equipment

Short boards mean different things to different people. A 290cm under a fifteen-stone man will be almost a sinker, while a small-framed woman weighing seven stones or a youth can float happily on a 270cm. It is wise to have enough reserve volume in your first short board to support you and the rig at rest. Following gybes and other manoeuvres, a 'marginal', unlike a total sinker, will afford you a few seconds in which to gather yourself and flip the rig. All short boards feel manoeuvrable to begin with, so opt for a slalom model that has the essential qualities of speed and early planing.

Wind

Sailing short boards in too little wind is excruciating, nor do they respond well to enormous sails ($6m^2$ plus). The sheer weight of the rig tends to sink the board rather than drive it forwards, while long booms overload the back and provoke spin-out. A solid force 5 blowing cross or cross onshore is an excellent training wind. You can launch out on a beam reach, the board planes without a whip and you can use a small, light and easily manageable sail of $5m^2$ or less.

There are few experiences quite as exhilarating as scudding over the waves on a short board. Good stance, controlled aggression and perseverance are the keys to short board excellence. Here, UK Mistral Champion Steve Keightley closes the slot, sheets in and prepares himself for a dynamic takeoff

The light-wind waterstart

Acertain law all too often decrees that the launching of the short board coincides with a sudden and unexplained dropping of the wind. Unless you are confident about your ability to waterstart every time, even in a failing breeze, alarms will go off in your head as soon as you drift out of your depth. Such a state of mind does not make for a very relaxed, enjoyable and productive sailing session.

Not so very long ago, before the discovery of the new sitting stance, high-set booms made light-wind waterstart techniques necessary in quite stiff breezes. But now that booms are tied at a sensible level, it is possible to throw the rig more upright and muster enough power from the sail to pop out of the water in eight knots of wind or less without having to adapt your technique – so long as that basic technique is sound.

There comes a time, however, when due to a slight miscalculation you will find yourself further out to sea than originally planned, with the sun setting and the sharks circling; you are prostrate beneath a rig which, despite your text-book efforts, refuses to pull you the whole way. Now is the time to panic, or calmly resort to your alternative light-wind technique.

Recalling the waterstart theory, your aim is to expose the maximum sail area to the wind by extending the arms and getting the rig as upright as possible, at the same time making yourself a small and compact bundle to lift out. That is sound advice. You are, however, limited by the length of your arms so, in order to push the rig higher, you are forced to change your grip on the rig.

By grabbing the base of the mast with the front hand and the foot of the sail with the back hand, you can not only balance the rig bolt upright but also bring your bottom, and therefore your centre of gravity, much closer to the board. Controlling both the rig and the position of the board in that position requires a fine touch. Only very quick and deft reactions will stop the rig being overpowered or falling back down to windward.

Practice

Since this skill was born out of freestyle, our old friend the long board is once again a most forgiving practice platform. Deft rig control is the key to the light-wind waterstart, so from your normal stance just squat or sit on the board; then, taking hold of the mast and the foot of the sail, control the board's destiny. Thereafter, from the same position, lower your bottom into the water and try rocking back up, keeping the board on course by making subtle fore and aft movements of the rig.

Back to the sharks: the short board's lack of volume up front is the source of some frustration. You must keep the rig and your weight forwards as you rise up to hold the board off the wind, but the weight of the rig combined with any pressure on the front foot tends to drive the nose under. Predict this by applying pressure to the back foot and by releasing the back hand as soon as you have rocked over the centreline, thereby unweighting the mastfoot and levelling the board out. Then move the front foot back behind the mast before sheeting in and bearing away.

The light-wind waterstart requires deft rig control and agility. The key lies in getting as close to the side of the board as possible

1 If you are tired of being shark bait and pumping furiously under the rig to stay afloat . . .

2 . . . swim in towards the mastfoot, release the front hand and grab the mast a couple of feet below the boom.

3 Keep swimming the rig upwind (towards the front of the board) to stop the board heading up, and transfer your back hand from the boom to the foot of the sail.

4 Manoeuvre the rig so that it is perpendicular to the board with the board itself lying across the wind. Swim in towards the mastfoot, lift the back foot on to the board about two feet behind the mast and place the front one just in front of the mast. Holding the rig bolt upright, bend your legs to the extreme, and rock up over your feet, throwing your whole body forwards over the centreline.

5 Having such an unstable hold of the rig, it is easy to get overpowered and drop it to leeward as you rock forwards. As soon as your weight is over the centreline stand up, let go of the foot of the sail and take hold of the boom. Pump the sail to generate some lift and forward movement, and adopt as normal a stance as is possible in the conditions.

The clew first waterstart

Equilibrium can desert you when you most need it; during the middle of a race, for example, or directly in the path of a gnarly, cresting wave. If, however, you can control the rig as you fall and then pop straight back up in the clew first position, you may salvage board, rig, limb and perhaps even the World Cup. In a less pressing situation, when the rig lands awkwardly, waterstarting clew first rules out the tiring and lengthy necessity of having to swim either the board or rig through 180 degrees.

As you might expect, your basic waterstart technique must be flawless before you can attempt the clew first variety; thereafter it is a case of adapting that technique and being wise to the following:

1 When clew first, the leech is a very unstable leading edge. It is crucial, therefore, to keep the sail open. If the leech is allowed to face directly into the wind the rig will be impossible to hold.

2 Anticipation is the key. You should be planning your clew first waterstart the moment you have passed the point of no return and concentrating on keeping the rig clear of the water. You should even be selecting the exact spot and the angle at which you fall in.

Your apprenticeship for this manoeuvre should include a lengthy session on a long board just sailing up and down clew first, getting used to the fact that the roles of your arms are reversed. Once you are happy sheeting in and out with the front hand, try lying down on the board and levering yourself back up by pulling down through the mastfoot with the back hand.

1 Following an overcooked gybe, throw the arms up as you fall in, to keep the rig full.

2 The sail will feel unstable clew first, so keep it open by sheeting out with what is now your front hand, keeping the board off the wind by bearing down through the mastfoot with your back hand.

3 Push the rig high, and lever down on your back hand being sure *not* to sheet with the front.

4 As soon as you are upright, release the back hand and . . .

5 . . . flip the rig in the normal way.

The short board carve gybe

Although the long board gybing technique can be employed quite successfully on short boards, the more dynamic performance characteristics of the latter highlight the need for a slightly modified technique.

Speed
With a few exceptions, short boards travel faster in relation to the wind than their longer cousins. To prevent them running away with you, you have to keep your weight further forwards on the board.

Smooth turning
Slalom and wave boards are built with gybing in mind. Increased rocker, curve in plan shape and 'V' in the tail are just some of the design features that allow more of the rail to be engaged in the gybe without the board stalling (some wave boards, like surf-boards, will turn around the rail's entire length). In a long, fast turn, this allows you to place the back foot further forwards, keep the board flatter and so maintain maximum speed.

As a result of both its speed and its

See how these slalom sailors have leaned their rigs into the turn as they carve around the mark. Raphael Salles and Nevin Sayre jostle for the inside slot

The short board carve gybe

turning ability, the short board, if trimmed properly, will happily carve through a complete arc with no help from the rig. Under windy circumstances, this allows you to release the rig well before the board has turned downwind.

Volume

As mentioned, due to the lack of volume a short board responds angrily to sudden foot movements. In this way, the foot change is a critical time since it upsets the trim and can stop the board carving. If you do it in the clew first position (as per long board) at a time when the board has lost most of its momentum, you effectively slam on the brakes, and while the rig is being flipped round you risk sinking without trace.

Speed through the turn is all-important. It lends you both time and stability. The key to fluid short board gybing lies in the technique of releasing the rig early when the board is travelling at its fastest, holding the board at a steady angle through the arc and not moving the feet until you have sheeted in and are planing fast on the new tack.

Ironing out the wrinkles

Snow skiing provides a useful comparison: if you lean back when trying to turn on a steep slope, the skis will accelerate off down the fall line giving you no choice but to sit down. Whereas if you push forwards in your boots and anticipate the course of the skis by leaning your upper body down the hill, you remain over your skis in a position to edge and control them.

It is the same on your short board. If you lean back, you can be in no position to dominate the board; but with your weight forwards and your knees flexible, you can drive the board through the water. Should it start bouncing over the chop, you can hold the edge in by flexing and extending the legs.

The next time you are standing on the tube or on a bus, try to keep your balance without hanging on. With straight legs the task is nearly impossible, but if you drop your centre of gravity and keep your back straight, you can relax and counteract the jerks and the swaying by simply throwing the knees from side to side and flexing the ankles.

The ultimate test comes when the train takes off from a station. To avoid being sent spinning to the back of the carriage, you must anticipate the acceleration by leaning the hips and then the knees forwards. The upper body position is also crucial. With the back still straight, suck your stomach up under your rib cage and throw your shoulders forwards. Your chest should be a concave shape. If you arch your back, the natural tendency is to fall back. Then, just close your eyes, extend your arms and imagine you are holding a boom.

Carving the board is fun and soon comes with committed practice, but perhaps the hardest element of the short board gybe is the rig release and catch. The stumbling block is your body's unwillingness to lean the rig to leeward into nothingness – something you might have done a hundred times before but never on purpose. Imagine that your UJ is solid. As the

1 Sailing on a beam reach, look and unhook! Place the back foot on the leeward rail, almost parallel with the front foot, facing the same direction, forwards and in.

5 Although the rig is de-powered, the knees stay bent with the body committed right inside. The old back hand now sweeps under and . . .

2 Bear away on to a broad reach and beware that the sudden acceleration does not leave you behind. Before carving, let yourself be pulled right forwards on the board until your knees, hips and upper body are over the centreline. Now commit the weight to the back foot . . .

3 . . . and drive the knees. Since you are not aiming to sink the tail, the direction of the drive can be more forwards. Note how the rig is upright and tilted right in to leeward. The arms are slightly bent to compensate for the fact that the sailor is so far forwards on the board.

4 Downwind, you must hold the angle and resist the urge to straighten up, which would in turn cause the board to scream off on a dead run. Due to the speed, the rig is now weightless, so prepare to throw it round with the back hand.

6 . . . grabs the front of the boom on the new side; the new back hand takes hold of the boom and prepares to sheet in.

7 As the power comes on, the feet are changed and slip straight into the straps. Note the low body position. With knees bent, you can immediately take weight off your feet and on to the rig to promote quick planing.

The short board carve gybe

As he banks the board over, the sailor leans the rig into the turn as if the UJ were locked solid, giving him a clear view of the front of the board

board banks over, the rig goes with it, so that there remains a constant ninety-degree angle between the deck and the mast. If you are doing it right you should be able to see the front of the board all the way through the gybe. If the sail obscures your view, you are guilty of 'scooping'.

The reason for holding the rig to leeward is that when the board has carved through the wind and it is time to sheet in on the new tack, the mast is actually hanging slightly to windward, so that you can take hold of the boom and sail away without having to make any adjustments.

The hand movements in the rig change are open to multiple interpretation. You may find it easier to go via the mast as displayed in the long board gybe; indeed, this method is preferable if you have lost a lot of speed, or you are overpowered. The slicker, swifter option is to go boom to boom, a feat that is easy so long as your board speed is good and you keep that vital distance between body and rig. The rig change now becomes a physical action as you actually throw the rig around and catch it on the new side.

Strong winds
As you would expect, things tend to happen a lot quicker in a strong-wind gybe. The board is travelling faster, the water surface is more ruffled, wind gets under the outside rail and tries to flip it over and it is easy to get overpowered, all of which demands very precise technique. Your reflexes during the carve must be sharp to keep the board banked, while the timing of the rig release

must be exact if you are to come out hooked in, strapped up and planing.

The greatest problem is undoubtedly the timing of the rig release. In winds of twenty five knots or less, you should be travelling at or near the wind speed when you bear away into the gybe. Downwind, therefore, the rig is weightless and you can stay sheeted in as the board swings through the turn. In winds over twenty five knots, it is not always possible to plane as fast as the wind. As you bear away, therefore, the sail can overpower you downwind. Either you get catapulted or the surge of power through the mast-foot causes the board to flatten out and trip over. There are two ways to control the power in this situation:

1 As you initiate the carve, oversheet. This effectively disrupts the airflow and de-powers the sail. At the same time, lay the rig right down to leeward, thereby exposing less sail area to the wind. This technique is like the first part of the carved 360° and is used by wave sailors during high-speed bottom turns.

2 Obtain your maximum controlled speed, start to bear away into the gybe, and, as soon as you begin to feel overpowered, release the rig and carve the board from reach to reach with the sail de-powered. Make a special effort to commit your weight inside and hold that angulated carving position, as the strong wind will try to blow you upright. Wait until the board has arrived on the new beam reach, and the apparent wind has flowed forwards, before trying to sheet in.

Speed control
In moderate winds, entering the gybe with insufficient board speed is, perhaps, the most common error, while in strong winds, attacking the manoeuvre at full throttle can also be disastrous. At top speed, the hull creates so much lift that you will struggle to make the rail bite. Such is one of the rare occasions that you must sheet out on entry to check your speed and make the board settle in the water before weighting the back foot and driving through with the knees.

The duck gybe

Hawaiian wave sailor Richard Whyte first duck gybed in the early 1980s. Within months 'duck fever' had gripped the world's beaches as every aspiring champion strived to conquer this outrageously difficult manoeuvre. Needless to say, if you were seen to have done one, you were lauded king of the beach.

Since that time, it has been discovered that the duck gybe is not so hard after all, and it has settled into its rightful position in the hierarchy of funboard manoeuvres. It was only difficult in that it all happened so quickly and no one was quite sure what they were supposed to be doing. In fact, it is a simple variation on the standard short board carve gybe, where instead of letting the sail swing round the front of the board, you

Carving the board hard, Robby Naish is about to throw the rig back over his left shoulder with his old front hand and 'duck' under the sail

throw the end of the boom over your head and 'duck' under the sail.

Its supposed advantage over the carve gybe is that the rig change occurs earlier, enabling you to use the sail to 'snap' out of the turn. In truth, a well-executed carve gybe produces much the same effect, and is preferred by slalom racers in critical situations, since you have better vision (in the duck gybe, the sail blankets your view ahead when you release it) and more

A very early version of the duck gybe performed by Mike Eskimo where the front hand grabbed the foot of the sail during the transition

The duck gybe

control during the approach to the mark.

The duck gybe is just one of the manoeuvres that makes short board sailing so varied and exciting. Performed well, it is a wonderfully fast and fluid turn and encourages you to widen and improve your board and rig handling skills. Surely those are reasons enough to give it a go!

In its purest form, the duck gybe is a high-speed turn during which the rig is redundant, apart from lending a touch of dynamism in the last act. So although the skill can be learned and practised on long boards, it is more suited to manoeuvrable short boards.

Quite rightly, it does score extra pose points and is an awe-inspiring trick to pull off in front of the clubhouse. People are tempted, therefore, to practise it before they have mas-

tered the basic carve gybe and, as a result, plummet relentlessly seawards in a flurry of arms and legs. Check your credentials before ducking away:

1 Are you entering your carve gybes with such speed that the rig becomes weightless downwind?

2 Are you in a position to release the rig early and still hold your carving position, and not change your feet until you have sheeted in on the new tack?

Many ways have been invented to get the hands from one side of the boom to the other. The first of these involved you going via the foot of the sail – some early surf sails even had a cloth handle there for that very purpose. However, it was usually in the wrong place and torn, bloodied fingernails were soon proof enough

that there had to be a better way. Indeed, the most practised technique today is an aggressive rig action that allows you to go straight from one side of the boom to the other.

Preparation

As with all funboard manoeuvres, success follows quickly if you know in which direction to channel your strength and enthusiasm. Trying a duck gybe is pointless until you have conditioned your body to that ducking feeling. To save hours of watery gymnastics, set the rig up on the beach or go out on a long board in light winds and familiarize yourself with the rig action. In freestyle terms it is a simple sail 180° to end up clew first. Once the rig change is automatic, wait for a force 4–5 and combine it with the basic carving action.

1 Approach the gybe at full tilt, look and unhook, bear away and initiate the carve in the normal way. When the board is on its fastest course and the rig feels light, shuffle the back hand towards the end of the boom.

2 Before the board faces dead downwind, cross the front hand over the back, grab the boom near the end and let the back hand go. The mast will swing down to leeward towards the water.

3 If you are totally committed inside, you should be able to stroke the water with your new front hand.

1 The rig has been released too early. The front of the boom has almost touched the water and the sailor has to bend at the waist if he has any hope of pulling it off.
2 Getting overpowered after the duck means that he either released the rig too late and tried to catch it on a run, or had insufficient board speed.

Speed and timing

Speed and timing are the two essential ingredients for the duck gybe. Slowing down to give yourself more time is disastrous since it allows the apparent wind to flow back and over-power you. When your board speed is roughly that of the wind, the rig is weightless and can be thrown effortlessly from one tack to the next. Remember, this is a carved turn so the board must have sufficient momentum to carry it all the way round.

Given that you must 'do the duck' on your fastest point of sailing, the timing of the rig release will depend very much on the wind strength. In moderate winds, you will be at top speed quite tight to the wind, perhaps just off a beam reach, so duck early. In stronger winds, your fastest course will be much broader, so duck late.

The symptoms of poor timing are easy to recognize: if you release the rig too early, the front of the sail is so powered up that the mast is blown down into the water to leeward (also the symptom of poor speed); too late and the sail backwinds as you release it, giving you no chance of getting to the other side of the boom. Keep the duck gybe for moderate to fresh winds (force 4–6); in gales, the rig swings around with such speed during the duck phase, and fills with such force when you sheet in again, that the manoeuvre looks and feels ungainly and perilous.

The rig change

The rig change must be aggressive. Many are those who have left teeth marks in the end of the boom, visible evidence of standing too upright, leaning back when releasing the rig and of not ducking!

Have one thought in mind when flipping the rig – to get your new front hand as far forwards on the new side of the boom as your arm length allows. If your hand lands in front of the balance point, you can immediately spill wind and bring the sail under control. The action that makes this possible even with long-boom sails is the vigorous pull-back action of the old front hand. You should throw the rig so far back over your head that you brush your shoulder with your ear. It is the sign of a fast, exciting sailing style that allows you to delay the duck until the very last moment, so that until you actually release the front hand, onlookers will not know which gybe you are about to execute.

4 Pull the boom back with the front hand and, still with the knees pushing forwards, duck under the sail and grab the new side of the boom with the new front hand as near to the mast as possible. Note how, despite the activity up top, the knees and feet keep the board carving at the same angle.

5 With the back hand on the boom, you now have the rig under control and can sheet in to maintain speed. Note that the board has hardly turned through the wind but you already have power back in the rig.

6 As the board carves round on to the new tack, swiftly change the feet, slipping them straight into the straps. You are now back in your most efficient stance having never dropped off the plane.

The slam gybe

This manoeuvre has been bestowed with a bewildering number of labels: 'sink', 'spin', 'scissor' and 'slam' have all been used to describe what is basically a very short-radius gybe, achieved by a dramatic sinking of the tail. As well as causing a lot of spray and turning a few heads, it does have practical applications:

1 Staying upwind on short boards often poses problems. The slam gybe is one of the safest and quickest ways of turning your board around without losing ground.

2 It is an invaluable weapon in slalom racing, allowing you to turn inside your rivals and hug the inside slot. And, on the start line, you must be able to manoeuvre quickly in tight spaces to avoid the mêlée.

3 Should the wind drop as you build up for a long, screaming, one-handed carve, the slam gybe is an ideal and equally dynamic alternative.

Although you can gybe long boards quite tightly in strong winds, their volume makes it hard to sink the tail enough to get that essential 'snap'. The authentic slam gybe, therefore, is for boards of 290cm and under.

Do not confuse a tight carve gybe with a slam gybe. Shortening the radius of the carve gybe is accomplished simply by increasing the pressure on the back foot, sinking the rail deeper and banking the board at a steeper angle. The slam gybe, meanwhile, is effectively a high-performance flare gybe, where rig power is used to turn the board about a pivot point, in this case the skeg.

Beware!

All the cardinal carve-gybing sins, such as scooping the rig, sinking the tail and straightening the front leg, are, ironically, the key points of the slam gybe. Consolidate your carve gybing skills before going for the 'slam' or risk having the former irreversibly corrupted.

1 With the mast located at the back of the track, approach on a close reach to check your speed, sheeting out a little if necessary. Bring your weight inboard, stand up over the centreline, look and unhook, and place the back foot well back on the leeward rail over the skeg.

2 Sit on your back foot, and drive the tail into the water with unbridled aggression; move the back hand a few inches further down the boom for better leverage and sheet in hard, scooping the rig slightly to windward. The legs perform a scissor action. The front leg kicks the board up and round while the back leg drags the tail under your bottom.

3 Check the upper body position. With the board pivoting so fast, it is easy to get flung to leeward, hence the need to hang your centre of gravity right to the inside of the circle, keeping the back straight. The board now snaps round and lands on the new reach. Stay very low, with your bottom almost in the water, to control the rig in the clew first position. See how the body leans forwards, hangs off the boom and applies pressure to the mastfoot to level the board out and 'kill' the rotation.

Practice ground

Ultimately you will be able to pull off a slam gybe in all winds. Due, however, to the fact that the board comes to a virtual standstill, the force in the sail immediately before and after the rig change is considerable. Ideal practice conditions, therefore, are those marginal winds (force 3–4) when there is not quite enough for good, clean carve gybes.

Perfecting the slam gybe in strong winds is one of the few windsurfing manoeuvres that asks you to grit your teeth and flex your biceps. One particularly good example springs to mind: during the slalom final in the Japan World Cup, in fifty knots of wind, Robby Naish was in second place approaching the final mark. The leader wisely approached the buoy from way upwind and carved a huge, long arc in an effort to control his speed and simply survive the turn. Despite the ferocious conditions, Naish saw the gap and managed to spin his board on its tail next to the mark, thereby landing upwind and yards ahead of his opponent. Such an effort required brutal strength to control the rig and split-second timing.

Success in such winds (preferably slightly less than fifty knots) requires total commitment and an exaggeration of all the movements. You have to sink the tail deeper to brake your speed (some go as far as to stamp on the tail with both feet), hang your upper body more to the inside, and, most importantly, hold the rig in tight. To resist the huge force in the sail as you pivot downwind, bend the arms and pull the rig down over your head, thereby exposing less of it to the wind. Moreover, in strong winds, the board will turn quite fast enough without the need for a big scoop of the rig. Just hold the rig upright and flip it round as soon as you have turned through the wind. *Do not* try to hold it clew first for any length of time.

4 Quickly change the feet, placing the front foot well forwards in front of the straps, and lever yourself upright by pulling down through the mastfoot with the old front arm (the one nearest the mast). *Do not* linger in the clew first position, as the rig will feel horribly unstable...

5 ... but flip it at once, changing the hands in the normal way. Make sure the mast is forwards and upright before releasing the back hand.

6 The board is prone to luffing at this stage, so bring the power back on immediately, bending the knees as you sheet in, to withstand the pull.

The aerial gybe

This acrobatic transition has rapidly become a favourite on inland and coastal venues. It does have a certain beach appeal. It is a nice one to execute in front of the clubhouse and the fact that it is actually a lot easier than it looks has persuaded many people to take to the air rather than master the faster carve and duck gybes.

The simple fact is that a small board will pivot round very easily in midair. The skill of the aerial gybe lies not so much in the aerial phase as in the subtle changing of the feet and a smooth landing. If you can 'chop hop' and can waterstart clew first, there is nothing to stop you trying this very enjoyable stunt.

Before gritting the teeth and bracing the knees, pause to consider what factors will help or hinder your attempts. Speed, so often the essential criterion for funboard manoeuvres, is actually far less important here than height. The change of direction takes place within the space of a few metres, so the faster you are moving in midair, the greater the shock on landing.

Bearing away, the normal procedure before any gybe, will also make life difficult; not only will your speed increase, but if you take off on a broad reach, you will land travelling sideways and place enormous strain on your fin and yourself.

The key to the aerial gybe is to head up into the wind immediately prior to takeoff so that, as near as possible, the board cartwheels vertically over its nose. The nose will touch down first, breaking the fall, and you will land stationary.

1 Take the back foot out of the strap, look for a steep piece of chop, head into the wind to meet it and lift up the front hand and the front foot.

2 Retract your heels to lift the skeg clear and then kick the tail right through the wind by extending the back leg.

3 At the top of the jump, change the feet into their new positions, placing them in front of their respective straps. Touch down nose first . . .

4 . . . and absorb the shock of landing by bending at the knees and waist. Note how the rig is held upright and forwards with straight arms to prevent the board luffing up.

5 Flip the rig as soon as you have regained control.

The foot change occurs at the top of the jump so that there is no twist on the knees on landing. Change the rig after landing, so that you have control during the flight and can steady yourself in the clew first position on splashdown.

During the first attempts, it is wise to land deliberately in the clew first waterstart position, with your weight off the board, in order to familiarize yourself with the shock of landing. But do not let it become a habit. If, every time, you land a long way from the board, you are guilty of taking off downwind and are getting left behind to windward.

Luffing and spin-out can also be the result of a downwind takeoff; alternatively, you might be landing too flat. As your jumps get higher and you have more time in the air, you should concentrate on drawing the board underneath you as soon as it has spun through 180 degrees. You should also remember always to hold the rig forwards.

The carve 360°

The 360° is a totally eccentric yet thoroughly enjoyable short board stunt. It seems like a lot of fuss to end up going in the same direction but it adds a touch of spice to your short board routine and can be pulled out equally on those windy, flat water days or on the face of a wave.

In theory it should be very easy. Instead of flattening the board out and flipping the rig as for a carve gybe, you simply keep leaning on the inside rail and continue carving until you end up where you started. Why then does it continue to baffle and frustrate hundreds of short board sailors?

Equipment plays a vital role in the classroom. Although you can sail through 360 degrees on any length of board, the manoeuvre in its proper form can only be performed on one under 290cm. Moreover, boards with flat rocker lines tend to stop carving after 180 degrees as their straight rails grab the water. Ideally, you should be using a wave-orientated board with some tail lift so that it will continue to carve even as it loses speed and starts to sink down in the water.

Conditions can also make the manoeuvre easy or impossible. Choppy water hinders a clean carving action, so practise on flat water, inshore, between waves, or on the wave itself. The ideal wind strength is force 5–6. Much more and, as with the basic carve gybe, your board speed does not match that of the wind and you risk losing control of the sail downwind. Moreover, it is easy to get overpowered in the front to sail position. Your best chance of success will be with a 5.3m^2–4.5m^2 sail.

Problems with the 360° are easier to analyse than to rectify. In various ways, people flop to the ocean before they get all the way round. Surprisingly, lack of pure speed is less often the correct diagnosis than poor weight distribution, the wrong turning circle and poor rig control.

It is crucial to maintain the same trim angle and keep the board carving on its tail. You might be tempted to bear away before banking over in order to lessen the distance you have to travel, but to do so is a mistake; downwind, the weight of the rig levels the board out, increases the waterline length and stops the board pivoting. Instead, start the carve on a beam reach when the board is planing on its minimum wetted area and aim to describe a tighter circle.

Applying a lot of pressure to the inside edge encourages the tail to sink as soon as the board comes off the plane, so bring the front foot out of the strap after about 180 degrees and place it well forwards near the mast-foot to keep the board level.

Despite the manoeuvre's name, it is very rare to carve the board on the plane all the way through the spin; suffice it to say that you will have to sail it through the last 120 degrees. This is the moment when so many relinquish the struggle. As you lay the rig down into the front to sail position, *do not* simply shove it to leeward with straight arms; the chances are that you will push the clew too far into the wind, stall and fall on top of the sail. Remember to lay the rig towards the back of the board and keep it open so that the sail can push the back of the board through the wind.

One of the best training toys for a 360° is a speed-sailor (a windsurfer on wheels). The board keeps rolling despite errors of trim, giving you all the time in the world to experiment with rig and body positions.

The carve 360°

1 Robby Naish begins this 360° by carving hard as if entering a tight gybe. His back foot is out of the strap, he is sheeted in and is leaning down on the rig.

2 Banking the board right over, maintaining his speed with a smooth carve and constant pressure on the back foot, he lays the rig right down to leeward, lifting up with the back hand and pushing down with the front hand.

3 As he approaches 180°, the board comes off the plane; so, in order to keep it level, he takes his front foot out of the strap and places it right forwards by the mastfoot.

4 He sweeps the sail behind him so that wind can drive the back of the board through the next section, being sure to keep the sail open and not push the clew through the wind.

5 As he comes head to wind, he anticipates the next phase by standing up and pulling the rig upright.

6 Finally, he falls back against the sail and bears away by sheeting in hard and pulling the tail of the board under his bottom with his back foot.

A fierce onshore wind turns the ocean into a cauldron of foam, makes it hard to get out and forces you to sail parallel with the waves

side' (facing the wave), is tricky since you find yourself on a dead run on the wave face and therefore seriously underpowered.

Cross shore winds combined with a good swell are the wave sailor's dream, allowing for the very best in jumps and riding. You can reach straight out through the waves and, with less chop build-up, the faces tend to be smoother and steeper for more radical jumps. Having 'dropped in', you can ride the wave equally well up or downwind, depending on which way it is breaking.

Cross offshore It is dangerous to advocate launching into any kind of offshore wind, especially on a short board, but the truth is that cross offshore winds blowing over a strong swell produce the best downwind wave riding conditions. The wind holds up the waves, so that they roll up in perfect sets, steep, polished and hollow. Jumping is a hit-and-miss affair as the wind is usually gusty especially in front of the faces, where the apparent wind created by the wave and the true wind cancel each other out to leave a large hole. When riding downwind, however, you have maximum power in the sail as you reach the lip which lays the ground for some spectacular aerial turns. In an emergency, you can at least make it back to land on one tack.

Direct offshore winds are wholly unsatisfactory and, for reasons mentioned in Chapter 7, potentially lethal. To jump, you would have to hit the waves on a dead run and when riding, if ever you managed to force the nose down a wave, the apparent wind would blow from so far forwards that the rig would be impotent.

Waves
The surf that rolls up the beach, the passage of the QE2 notwithstanding, comes in the form of either windblown waves, or a swell.

Windblown waves are the result of a local weather system and arrive and disappear with the wind. Their size and frequency will depend on the wind's strength and the fetch – the distance between the beach and the windward shore. The longer the fetch, the better spaced they are. Regrettably, windblown waves are all most beaches can hope for and, while offering reasonable jumping ramps, they are usually too mushy and unpredictable for good wave riding.

Choosing the conditions

Swell is produced by violent storms hundreds, often thousands of miles away over a foreign seaboard; therefore, it only rolls up on beaches that face out into open ocean. By studying the weather chart and noting the depth and position of distant depressions, surfers can predict the size and direction of the waves and their likely time of arrival. During their passage across the ocean, they form into well-defined sets, ideal for surfing, wave riding and jumping. They are characteristically more powerful and more predictable, peeling left or right down their whole length, rather than crumbling. Since they have nothing to do with the local weather, it is possible to find a good swell with a sideshore wind.

The beach
It often occurs that while one beach is unsailable, another less than a mile away will be entertaining perfect six-foot waves. Such contrasting conditions are usually brought about by the beach's aspect and the shape of the sea bed.

The Hawaiian Islands boast such gargantuan rollers due to the fact that they have no continental shelf. The huge swells roll along in water several miles deep, when suddenly they are forced over the coral reefs less then ten feet below the surface. Energy stored over thousands of miles is suddenly crammed into a tiny space, causing the wave to peak vertically, overtake itself and form those famous 'barrels' or 'tubes'.

On a smaller scale, the same effect can be seen when normal waves hit sandbanks or submerged rocks. If the wave is forced into shallow water it will often 'dump' or 'close out' (break at once down its entire length), but if the water is deep enough, it will simply steepen and become ideal fodder for the wave rider.

As the tide rises and falls, the wave conditions will continually change. On a number of beaches, a history of storms has caused sand and shingle to heap up and form a shelf by the high-tide mark. At high tide, therefore, the waves mount that shelf and crash on the bank. Many a brave windsurfer has been lost in the rinse cycle attempting to launch against such odds. As the tide recedes, however, dropping away on to the flat sea bed, the waves enter the shallow water gradually and so peak and break more gently.

Close out conditions, where the wave jacks up and then breaks along its entire length without peeling, are a nightmare for the wave sailor. Steve Keightley woke up from this dream with a broken mast

Jumping techniques

Like it or not, you will end up airborne if you sail in waves. It is the inevitable result of a projectile hitting a ramp at about 32kph/20mph. It is important to master the art of in-flight control, or else you risk spending an unhealthy amount of time floundering in the foam.

The chop hop

Ironically, you do not need waves to learn to wave jump. With a strong wind, a degree of skill and a board under 3 metres, you can get some impressive air time off a piece of chop within the sanctity of your local pond. Jumping technique relies on turning your forward momentum into height and using the airfoil qualities of your sail to suspend you and help you complete a smooth touchdown.

In order to create that essential lift, you must take advantage of every power source available to you.

Your legs Connected to the board by the footstraps, the legs can physically lift the board out of the water. It is also through their push-pull action that you control the direction of flight.

Your arms, via the boom and the mast, are in contact with the mastfoot. By pulling up with the front arm, you can lift the mastfoot and direct the nose of the board skywards. Your back arm, as when sailing normally, controls the sail's power, so by sheeting in vigorously you can generate an extra surge of power and lift.

The wind You must encourage the wind to blow under the board and sail so that the rig can act like a wing. By bringing it down to windward over your head after takeoff, you turn the forward force into lift.

Timing

You can kick the legs and pump the arms frantically in the gale of the year, but unless they all work at the same moment, the board will stick to the water like a limpet. Some experts can execute the most outrageous jumps off the tiniest waves with apparent ease, simply because they channel all the forces available into one dynamic moment. More specifically, they time their effort on the top of a steep piece of chop so that they lift, kick and pump when just the tail is in contact with the water.

Chop is the direct result of the wind on the water. If you are constantly

Tail first landing

1 On a reach at full planing speed, when you see a steep piece of chop, carve upwind towards it and, as the nose mounts the face, lift up with the front hand and the front leg, drawing a deep breath to make yourself as light as possible, and take the weight off the board.

2 Sheet in hard, lift the windward rail and let the wind blow under the board. Note that the stance, even in the air, remains uncorrupted, with the head looking forwards over the front shoulder, the shoulders parallel to the sail, the arms straight, the hands well down the boom shoulder-width apart and the bottom dropped.

3 Now bear the board away by drawing the back of the board up under your bottom with the back foot and stretching out the front foot with a scissor action. Stay sheeted in.

4 For a tail first landing, extend the back foot towards the water and bend both knees to absorb the shock.

Jumping techniques

aware of the wind direction, you may find that a sudden shift allows you to meet the chop head-on rather than side-on and so gain more height.

Landing
Taking off is one thing, landing in control and sailing on unruffled is quite another. To preserve your knees and other joints, you must stop closing your eyes as soon as the board leaves the water, and endeavour to spot the runway and lower your undercarriage in good time. There are three ways to land a board:

1 Flat In all bar a few special cases where the jump is long and shallow and you want to maintain maximum speed (e.g. slalom), landing flat shatters boards, cartilages and morales and is not to be recommended.

2 Tail first is the safest and easiest way to come down. On contact with the water, the tail sinks and absorbs the shock of landing. However, the board does tend to lose a lot of speed.

3 Nose first is more spectacular, more challenging, more rewarding and infinitely more hazardous. The nose's volume allows the board to rock back down on to the water without sinking and maintain its forward momentum. If the foot movement is right, you can come down almost vertically and still bottom out. But if your timing is off and the approach a little too steep, the act ends suddenly and dramatically.

Problems
Undoubtedly the highest hurdle to overcome when learning to jump is learning to control the board's natural tendency to luff into the wind. As

soon as the skeg(s) fly clear, their lateral resistance disappears and your feet push the tail away. The effect is often exacerbated by pilot error:

Sheeting out as you lift off might feel like a safe thing to do but it just causes the sail to luff and the CE to move back, and increases the pressure on the tail. Keep the power on all the way through the jump.

Straight legs limit your in-flight control, if indeed you get airborne at all. You must lift your heels, which not only gives you height but also draws the tail into the wind.

Spin-out on landing from jumps big and small is often caused by exerting too much pressure on the fin. Try to touch down with the nose just downwind of the tail to reduce that sudden lateral pressure, and land with your weight equally on both feet, taking some of the force on the rig.

Nose first landing
1 Approach the jump as before, going for maximum height off a small wave.

2 Lift the heels and draw the board right underneath you so that your bottom hangs over the windward rail. If you are flying for a while, the weight of the rig pushing down through the mastfoot naturally flattens the board off and sends the nose plummeting.

3 To steepen the dive on small jumps, increase the mastfoot pressure by extending the front arm slightly and sheeting in hard. Look at the water ahead and anticipate the impact.

4 On shallow dives, if the board has sufficient rocker it will bottom out. If the approach is radical, the moment the nose touches the water, extend the back leg to stop it pearling.

Variations on a theme

Stefan van den Berg sails his board through this long jump. He sheets in, stays compact, drops his weight down to windward and controls the angle of the board with his toes and ankles

Having consolidated your basic jumping skills on flat or choppy water, you are suitably armed to head for the more extreme launch pads in and around the white water. The types of jump you can hope to achieve will depend ultimately on your gymnastic ability, your spacial awareness, your foolhardiness and, of course, the strength of the wind and the size and steepness of the ramp in front of you.

Long jumps

You would be well advised to go for your first jumps on the small re-formed waves close to the beach. They arrive in the shape of tumbling white water or gentle unbroken lumps, but in both cases they will be

The 'donkey kick' is the first progression on the way to the illustrious 'table top'

131

Variations on a theme

quite small, knee to waist height, with shallow faces to launch you along rather than vertically upwards.

Long jumps get you used to being in the air for a longer period of time and allow you to practise trimming the sail and the board while the right way up. It is not only an excellent feeling to be floating a few feet above the sea in your normal sailing position, relaxed, comfortable, surveying the surroundings, but this style of jump is perfected by slalom racers who need to maintain a low, flat trajectory in order to land at full speed on the plane.

The basic skill is much the same as

for the chop hop except that you do not have to luff up to meet the wave. So long as the wind is not straight onshore, you can afford to bear away to accelerate as the wave approaches. To lift the nose over the white water, increase the pressure on the back foot as it starts the climb, before lifting the heels the moment the skegs come clear. Make that back-foot pressure as subtle as possible to avoid sinking the tail and stalling. To delay landing and to prevent the board from following its favourite path into the wind, stay small and compact, hold the power in the sail, hanging your weight right down below the windward rail, and

push the nose downwind with the front foot. Remember, your stance on the board should be the same in mid-air as it is on the water.

Donkey kicks

From this point forwards the only goals are to impress, stretch the imagination to the limits, defy gravity and somehow avoid injury. The donkey kick is one of the easier ways of lending your basic jumps a touch of flair, and is the first step towards getting totally inverted.

The donkey kick, as the name suggests, involves you kicking the board out to one side, and then retracting it quickly under your body again. A steeper wave is required to help you throw the board out sideways and give you enough time to bring it down. Bear away as the wave approaches and, as soon as the skeg flies clear, instead of drawing the tail under your bottom, kick it out into the wind by straightening the legs out sideways and by angulating at the waist. It helps to lean your upper body slightly to leeward and hang off the boom with straight arms. At the apex of the jump, pull the board beneath you and bend your legs for a tail first landing. Only if the jump has been exceptionally high can you control the board in time to touch down nose first.

Problems

With this and other totally or partially inverted jumps, the main cause of a

Robby Naish displays both
suppleness and dynamism as he
soars into a classic table top

splash-landing is failure to have the board in landing mode at the crucial moment. In the case of the donkey kick, unless you redirect the board as you drop, you will land dead downwind only to be overpowered as soon as you touch the water. To give yourself more time, start to kick the tail into the wind even as it is mounting the wave face and retract it again the moment it starts its descent.

Upside down

The 'table top' jump, so named because the underside of your board faces the sky in the position to support a couple of glasses, is fabulously spectacular, not just because first attempts so often culminate in a parting of board and rider, often some way above the ocean. If the wave is the right shape, it is quite easy to attain the desired position. However, spacial awareness, that valuable asset of knowing exactly where you are at any given moment in time and space, often deserts you when you most need it, giving you no other choice but to pull the ripcord.

There are two ways of getting upside down. The first method involves taking the donkey kick a stage further; that is to say, kick the tail into the wind and invert it to the side and over your head by bending the knees and arching the back. For the most extreme contortions, it helps to sheet out a little at the apex of the jump. Alternatively, by pulling back violently on the rig, and lifting up with both feet keeping the legs extended, you can bring the board straight over your head as if performing the first half of a straight-back

somersault. The finishing touch is a 'tip dip', where the tip of the mast catches the crest of the wave.

Both variations, especially the latter, require a vertical wave face. Therefore, watch the wave pattern to see where the waves are peaking. Then time your run, bearing away if necessary, so that you hit the steepest section just before it breaks.

Landing successfully from the most outrageous positions is quite feasible. Rig pressure on the mastfoot naturally levels the board out in midair, even when upside down, from where you use your feet to angle the board just off the wind for splashdown.

Bailing out

There are many times during your training flights when discretion should be the better part of valour. If you feel uncomfortable up there, have lost control or are getting altitude sickness, then *bail out!* When ejecting, make sure you throw board and rig downwind as far away from you as possible.

At other times, you may be in control but have noticed that the altimeter is off the clock; you then begin to fear for the wellbeing of your board and joints. To soften the impact of landing, pull the rig over your head, hang your bottom below the windward rail and aim to land in the waterstart position. It is preferable to bailing out for the simple reason that you do not have to swim after your rig in the breaking surf.

Looping

They said it was physically impossible. But when Doug Hunt of Maui (Hawaii) broke the credibility barrier by completing a full back somersault with board and rig, within months hundreds of wave sailors were spinning above the ocean the world over.

The loop is not a manoeuvre that lends itself to structured practice and analysis for it relies on eighty per cent commitment and twenty per cent skill. Before you 'go for it', you should at least be able to land nose first and do good upside down jumps. Thereafter, it is a case of controlled aggression and trying to keep a cool head in the face of considerable danger.

The backward loop

The backward loop is the first and most natural of the aerial somersaults. Natural, however, only insofar as the board is already heading in that direction as it climbs the face of the wave. There are two variations on the manoeuvre: the loop itself in its purest form where the nose passes vertically over the tail, and the barrel roll where board, rig and sailor roll over diagonally into the wind. The loop is infinitely more difficult and requires a big wave and a lot of speed since the board must be at least fifteen feet above the water to allow the mast tip to clear the waves. The barrel roll, on the other hand, has been performed on lakes off the wake of motorboats.

Landing

Performing a 360-degree turn in the air is easy compared to the messy business of landing. Out of one hundred attempts, the pioneering 'looper' would be happy to sail away from one. Today the success rate is better, although not even the best can profess to do it every time. The problem lies in the ever-changing conditions. No one ramp is the same. The speed of approach varies with the wind, and there is no telling whether it will gust or drop in mid-manoeuvre.

First attempts

Select a steep wave no more than head height for your first attempt. With a cross, or cross offshore wind, you can complete nearly 90 degrees of the turn before the skeg has left the water by carving hard into the wind as you climb the face.

As you lift off, lift up with the front hand as if doing an overhead jump and kick the board over the front shoulder. Stay sheeted in and compact all the way round. The head is very much the leader. Throw it back and the rest of the body will follow.

Reasons for *not* completing a barrel roll are many and varied. Apart from basic fear and lack of commitment, the most common way of coming to grief is through over-rotation and luffing into the wind the moment you land. Indeed, the larger the wave and the more height you get, the greater your chances of completing one and a half somersaults and of crashing violently.

Only experience and a number of failures can teach you to control the rate at which you revolve in the air. That recurring theme of spacial awareness is once again the key issue. To help you stay orientated in your upside-down world, employ the same technique as gymnasts and acrobats and try as soon as possible to spot your landing. In this case that means throwing your head over your front shoulder and trying to focus on the water beneath you. Off high jumps, some of the best exponents of the art such as Matt Schweitzer and Peter Cabrinha have developed a technique of delaying the loop halfway in the upside-down position, thereby slowing the rotation. As they start to drop, they twist out backwards with much more control.

The forward loop

The forward loop is a more recent

1 Robby Naish performs this barrel roll in cross onshore winds off only a head-high wave. He initiates the rotation by carving into the wind up the face.

In onshore winds, where the waves are often slow and mushy, good board speed is needed to produce an explosive riding performance. Here in some hostile Dutch North Sea soup, Naish executes his favourite 'aerial backside off-the-lip'

Anders Bringdal flips the rig as he gybes off the lip. He can shorten the radius of the turn, knowing that the wave will provide the acceleration

lip is a 180-degree pivot where the board is projected vertically up the face to be 'cracked' round by the pitching lip. As the lip hits the underside of the board, the sailor leans right back and extends his back leg, forcing the inside of the tail into the water. Carving hard with the back heel, he then sheets in to snap the board right round. The drop back down the wave will also be vertical, so he keeps his weight back to avoid pearling.

The timing is critical: too early and the board could stall, too late and you will either just flop off the back of the wave, or be engulfed by white water.

The wind direction ultimately decides how dynamic your top turns will be. Cross offshore is the best direction as you arrive at the crest with maximum power in the sail. If the wind is just slightly onshore, you find yourself almost dead downwind

as you try to pivot, in a position where it is easy to oversheet and stall the sail. The key to good top turns in the less favourable wind directions is speed. The faster you are moving along the wave face, the more the apparent wind moves forwards and the greater the drive in the sail.

If you are sailing in little wind or find yourself underpowered as you reach the top of the wave, move your back hand more into the middle of the boom nearer the balance point, so that as you sheet in you will simply increase the airflow rather than drag the clew through the wind.

Backside The top turn and off-the-lip with your back to the wave are less dynamic, since you arrive at the top of the wave almost into the wind and with no power in the sail. The turn is completed solely with a foot-carving action. Head to the wind, with the

back foot right over the tail, weight the leeward rail, sheet out and lean forwards into the sail to direct the board down the face. The dynamism factor again depends on your bottom turn, and on the speed at which you hit the lip.

The aerial off-the-lip is a superbly spectacular, very risky manoeuvre which scores very highly in wave contests. It requires perfect timing so that as the lip lifts the board round, you sheet in hard, lift the heels and fly off the top to land in the trough ready to lean into another bottom turn. The problem lies in controlling the flight. It is difficult controlling the rig since the air immediately around the wave face is very disturbed. Moreover, landing from a height on to white, aerated water often results in spin-out. Attempt to land without too much weight on the back foot.

Chapter 12 WINDSURFING COMPETITIONS

Racing offers enormous excitement to windsurfers of all standards and, as a means to improve your speed, your board handling, your awareness of the wind and your knowledge of board and rig design, it is unparalleled. There are those to whom the very notion of competition appears totally contradictory to the freedom and enjoyment that are windsurfing's trademarks. However, many enjoy the spirit of camaraderie inspired by the occasion, as fleets of like-minded sailors gather to get the best out of an afternoon and pit their wits and skills against nature as well as their fellow competitors. During a race your resourcefulness is put to the test: you have to sail to specific points, perform your tacks and gybes often on the choppiest water and you are for ever having to manoeuvre, either to avoid other competitors or to make best use of the current or the wind. Success does not depend on winning, but on achieving.

Types of competition

The running 'Le Mans' start is not strictly the fairest way to begin a slalom race, but the spectator appeal is undeniable

There are competitions today to cater for every conceivable discipline and level of ability. Most clubs host their own race series, and it is there that you can learn the basic rules and then use them to gain a tactical advantage. Thereafter you can enter any number of national events depending on the board you want to use and the type of course you would like to sail around.

One class design
Almost without exception, the world's top competitors started racing in a one class design fleet. The most active in the world are Windsurfer and Mistral. The advantage is that you require just one board and one rig and, with everyone using identical equipment, the best sailor wins, not the one with the biggest cheque book.

Division II
In 1988, windsurfers from all countries will compete for Olympic glory on Division II boards around the standard Olympic triangle course as used by the dinghy classes. Since the arrival of high-performance long funboards, the Division II fleets have

waned in some parts of the world while growing to vast proportions in others such as France. The expense and fragility of the boards are drawbacks, as is the course itself which includes a run downwind.

Division I
Division I was formed to give windsurfers a chance to compete at a high level on inexpensive, 'off-the-shelf' equipment. The original spirit has since disappeared as some have started building exotic custom boards to exploit the measurement rules (devised originally to exclude displacement hulls) to the full.

Funboard racing
Funboard racing represents a departure from tradition insofar as the emphasis lies on board handling skills rather than tactics. The rules have been simplified and the courses designed primarily to make windsurfing more of a spectacular sport; and secondly, to complement the reaching performance of the funboards themselves. The regattas take place in a minimum wind strength of eleven knots (force 4) and are run, conditions permitting, over three disciplines: course racing round a modified triangle course, slalom over a reaching course and wave performance.

Racing skills and equipment

Strangely, the most naturally-gifted windsurfers are not always the winners. Success in windsurfing at all levels is due partly to the man and partly to the machine. They do not necessarily have to be the very best but both must be finely tuned and in tune with each other.

Tuning the equipment

Champions are meticulous about their equipment. By attending to every detail, they not only improve their board speed but also start the race in the knowledge that they are 100 per cent efficient. They can concentrate on the race itself, free from nagging concerns that something might break.

Pre-match preparation involves making a number of tiny adjustments, none of which on their own would seem to make a big difference but which can add up to give you the edge.

The board

Water sticks to a glossy surface, while scratches and abrasions cause turbulence and drag. Present a smooth, clean surface to the water by going over the underside with rubbing compound or very fine wet and dry sandpaper. Be sure to sharpen up, not round off, the water release edges.

If you are going to race in planing conditions, a slot flusher is essential. An uncovered daggerboard slot is akin to towing a bucket. The torrent of water that pours out on to the deck is a physical manifestation of lost energy. The majority of long funboards have them as standard, usually made of rubber. Traditionally, it is an area brimming with problems. They can rip off, get trapped and jam the dag-

gerboard. They can be too soft to keep the water out of the case and can provoke spin-out by channelling air on to the fin. Check yours thoroughly, trimming down the edges if necessary. If your board is lacking one altogether, two strips of stiff mylar work well if you can find a strong enough contact adhesive.

The fin, as mentioned in Chapter 3, is an unheralded source of speed. At times, even on a long board, it represents a sizeable percentage of the wetted area, so choose one that is large

Your sail should be a creaseless foil — improved laminar flow will increase your board speed

and stiff enough to cope with your weight and the severe lateral forces exerted by a large racing sail. Check the foil for abrasions and, if you are happy with its performance, fill up the remainder of the fin box either with a silicone gel or an elastic padding to reduce the turbulence and your chances of spinning out.

On the deck, the non-slip surface

In order to bring the tack of the sail as close to the deck as possible, it is wise to discard your pulley hook

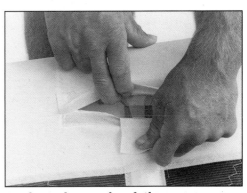

Sticky inducers that fail to rotate can exert a dramatic influence during tacks and gybes, so check that yours move freely on the mast

Racing skills and equipment

must be good if you are to find an efficient stance and manoeuvre comfortably. The footstraps must be adjusted so that you can hang your heel over the dome of the deck and push against the foils (the fin and the daggerboard).

The rig

The smoother the profile of your rigged sail, the more power it will generate. Apart from eliminating the creases, there are a number of small tuning tips that can result in yet more power.

In order to close the 'slot' right off, you must rig the tack of the sail as close to the deck as possible. Do away with your pulley block so that the cringle almost touches the cleat and, to bring it down yet further, invest in a downhaul cleat that hangs down parallel to the UJ on the mast extension. Many racing sails now have their tack cringles fitted a few inches up the luff, so that the foot of the sail can actually rest on the deck.

Camber inducers have a habit of sticking to, or falling off the mast. Check that they are properly seated. If they are not rotating freely, trim them down to fit the mast exactly.

The inhaul connection must be rock solid so that you can take your weight on the boom. To make a perfectly smooth leading edge, place a cover over the cut-out in the luff.

Harness lines require special attention. If you have to fight to hook in after every manoeuvre you will forfeit energy and places. To stop them wearing and to help them hang in an even loop, many racers thread the rope through plastic tubing. Fuel piping designed for farm vehicles is ideal. Remember always to get out on to the water in good time to adjust the lines for the sail and the wind strength. It will be impossible to have them positioned correctly for both reaching and beating. As a general rule, set them for reaching. Your back hand may have to work a bit to keep the sail sheeted in as the CE flows

back upwind; but if the line is too far back, you will oversheet as soon as you fall against the sail, your front arm will get overloaded and you risk being catapulted forwards.

Board speed

Having the very best equipment is only an advantage if you are familiar with it. Most racers agree that through constant practice, they will be sailing the same board as much as twenty five per cent faster at the end of the season than at the beginning – more than two legs of the course in distance terms. All good racers settle into a good stance but the winner is the one who is most sensitive to the needs of his board and rig. Training sessions are a time both for experimentation and for analysis.

On the reach:

1 Does the board feel more comfortable being sailed flat or does it pick up when heeled slightly to windward? This will depend on the number of concaves. Triple and double concave

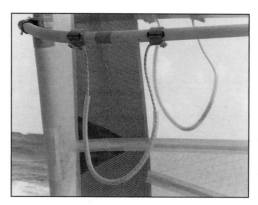

A cover that fits over the boom cut-out reduces turbulence around the mast and, after a fall, stops water pouring into the luff tube

Many metres can be lost if you have to fight to hook into floppy, twisted harness lines. Plastic tubing over stiff rope produces an even loop

To stop the leech opening prematurely, the clew must be locked to the end of the boom. A micro-adjustable back end is very convenient

As all the sailors fight for pole position down the first leg of the World Cup slalom in San Francisco, note the contrasting styles of Raphael Salles on the far left, who is railing his board and sailing it on one concave, and Nevin Sayre on the far right who is sailing his flat

boards often plane faster with just one concave in contact with the water.

2 In which set of footstraps do you feel most comfortable? By lengthening your harness lines and sailing with straighter arms, perhaps you can move into the back set earlier to reduce the wetted area.

3 Can you sail with the mast-track right back even in marginal planing conditions? If the reach is very broad and you feel the tail is dragging a little, move it forwards slightly to maintain the same trim angle.

4 Does the rig feel too full on the tighter reaches and does it seem to be causing drag? Are you sheeted in enough? People forget what a physical business racing is. You should always be pulling on the back hand, not so much as to oversheet and stall, but just enough to force more air over the sail. Harness line length is critical. A few inches too long and you are taking all the weight on your arms, too short and you risk either being pulled off your feet, or cranking the rig over to windward. To feel the wind shifts, have them no wider than shoulder-width apart.

Upwind technique

Since course races are more or less decided on the first beat, your upwind performance is crucial. Sailing upwind with the daggerboard down, especially in a blow, is a supreme test of sailing skill. The board travels slower upwind than on the reaches, so the lateral forces in the sail are greater. It is a fine balancing act as you have to correlate those forces with the lifting effect of the daggerboard by subtle weight distribution between feet and mastfoot.

Railing All boards point higher upwind if the leeward edge is engaged in the water and the board is railed to windward. This has the effect of:

1 improving the angle of attack of the daggerboard.

2 reducing the wetted area while maintaining waterline length.

3 increasing the lateral resistance. The full length of the leeward edge acts like a daggerboard.

4 keeping the board on the wind. If you were to depress the windward rail, the board would constantly bear away.

The extent to which you rail the board depends on the hull shape.

Anders Bringdal wins a course race in La Torche. Down the reaches he sails the board from the tail, and applies pressure to the fin to create lift and minimize the wetted area

Racing skills and equipment

Course races are usually decided on the upwind leg, so beating stance is crucial. The sailor encourages the board to rail by leaning forwards on to the mastfoot, and then controls the heeling angle through foot pressure on the windward rail

Round displacement hulls are sailed almost on the edge, while on funboards the action should be less extreme. Like on the reaches, it is a question of feel. You instantly know when the board is happy. If you 'over-rail', the footstraps drag in the water and the board constantly luffs. If you sail it too flat, it can feel directionally unstable.

In sub-planing winds, the railing effect is achieved simply by back-foot pressure on the leeward side. In stronger winds it is the daggerboard's lift that heels the board over. To help the board rail up, you simply take all your weight on the rig and then, to control that lift and prevent capsizing, you move both feet outboard on to the windward rail, shifting the weight between the rig and the feet to maintain the same angle. How you position your feet on the rail is vital. As you sheet in, your feet should apply pressure directly against the daggerboard, but if the foot is wrongly placed, the heel can simply flip the rail right over.

Many funboards have a set of beating straps and, although they might be well-placed for some conditions, *do not* be ruled by them. It is essential to be mobile to cope with waves and the other lifting forces. Many sailors keep their back foot still while their front foot floats up and down the rail, applying pressure when needed either to hold the rail down or bear the board away slightly.

Mast-track and daggerboard

The relationship between mast-track and daggerboard determines how easily the board will rail up and the ease of control in all wind strengths.

The basic rule is that the nearer the CE is to the CLR, the greater the lift from the dagger. In light to marginal winds, therefore, locate the track quite far back. As the wind strengthens, that lift becomes uncontrollable and will cause incurable luffing problems. Rather than retract the dagger, which will ruin your pointing ability, slide the track forwards. This moves the CE forwards which helps keep the nose off the wind as well as increasing the waterline length and lateral resistance. With the track too far forwards, the board ploughs through the waves and is reluctant to plane on the foil. Ultimately, everything depends on your weight, the state of the water and the strength of the wind.

If the wind is up during the race, the track/dagger formula is straightforward – right back and retracted for the reaches, forwards and down for the beats. On the reaches, however, where the wind is on the light side and unpredictable, hundreds of yards can be gained if you keep planing. Under these circumstances, the dagger can be an invaluable source of speed. By locating the track centrally and partially retracting the plate you can use the foil area to lift you on to the plane. Once the board is planing, and the airflow has established itself over the sail, you can retract it to reduce drag. Leaving the track some way forwards in marginal conditions helps to keep the board level.

Pumping

Although the action of 'pumping' the sail is still governed by some very

Course racing

vague, unenforceable rules (only three pumps per wave in Olympic-style IYRU regattas), it is now accepted in funboard circles as a skilful windsurfing technique rather than a way of cheating. Pumping is a way of speeding up the airflow over the sail – of creating your own wind and generating more power.

In light winds the action is like one of gathering air in a pillow case and then throwing it away behind you. It is easy enough to produce that initial drive by simply pulling in on the sail; the art lies in getting rid of that air and throwing the rig forwards again without the sail backwinding and driving you backwards. See your sail as a rower's blade. He closes it as he pushes it forwards through the air and then opens it up as he pulls it back through the water. If ever the sail flaps, you know immediately that the forces are working against you.

In stronger winds pumping should only be used to promote planing. Once the board is planing, the most efficient position for the rig is upright and still. It is like driving a car where you need a lot of energy to make it accelerate, but once you have reached your cruising speed, you can throttle back. The pumping action now involves the whole body. You use the rig as a means to support your weight while you shoot your hips and legs forwards. Instead of sheeting in and out, you pull down on the rig with straight arms, powering the board forwards through the mastfoot and pushing against your fin or dagger-board for extra lift. As the board accelerates, lift and rock the board to feed air into the concaves.

Although perhaps the least spectacular, course racing is the most complete racing discipline, since you are asked to perform on all points of sailing, tack, gybe, manoeuvre within a big fleet and maintain concentration for an hour or more. How you plan the race will be affected by the wind strength, the length of the course and the position of the buoys, the number of competitors, and the direction of the tidal stream – just a few of the variables that will influence your strategy.

Preparation

Having found out the rules to which the regatta is being run (Can you hit the marks? Is pumping allowed? etc.), rig up early to give you plenty of time to get out on the water beforehand to warm up, check the sail size, the harness line position and the position of the buoys, and to familiarize yourself with the wind and the new surroundings. If you arrive late and have to sail straight out to the start line, you will be at a huge disadvantage both mentally and physically.

The start

The preparatory signals vary from regatta to regatta although a popular sequence is:

> 6 minutes: class flag raised with sound signal.
> 3 minutes: three-minute or Blue Peter flag raised with sound signal.
> 1 minute: one-minute flag with sound signal.
> Go!: sound signal, all flags lowered.

Variations include a ten, five, one-minute sequence (generally considered to be unnecessarily long for windsurfers).

It is impossible to stress the importance of a clean start; suffice it to say that once a good sailor opens up a lead, he can control the race and will be difficult to pass.

Which end of the line?

Having arrived at the line in good time, your first job is to discover if the line has a port or starboard bias. In theory the line should be set exactly at right angles to the wind, although

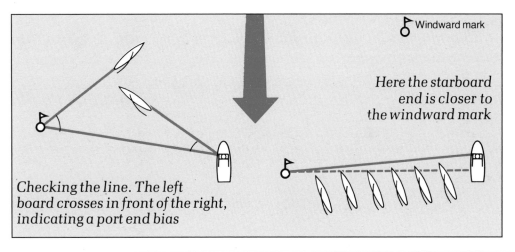

Checking the line. The left board crosses in front of the right, indicating a port end bias

Here the starboard end is closer to the windward mark

Windward mark

Course racing

sudden changes in the wind direction and the problems of mooring the committee boat mean that this is rarely the case. Basically you must aim to start at the end nearest the windward mark. There are a number of ways of finding out which way the line is slanted.

1 Line the board up on the start line, hold the uphaul rope and the end of the boom will point nearest to the favoured end.

2 Reach up and down the line. You are sailing towards the best end when on the tighter reach.

3 With a friend of similar standard, set off at either end of the line close hauled before the start and see who crosses over in front of who.

If the line is heavily biased, the fleet will quickly bunch up at one end. Under such circumstances pile-ups are commonplace, especially in the lee of the committee boat at the star-

board end. It often pays to sacrifice a little distance and head for uncluttered space further down the line.

Port or starboard?

If you start on port tack, you have to give way immediately to the rest of the fleet. Only on very rare occasions when a dramatic wind shift changes the bias will you be able to cross the whole fleet. If you do manage it, you take a commanding lead.

Clean air

If the line is crowded and no one end is particularly favoured, your one concern is to find a gap in the line. Using good board control, holding the board in one place and keeping the windward boards at bay, try to make a hole for yourself to leeward, so that at the gun you have room to bear away and accelerate. If you start in the shadow of a number of boards, you have to spend the rest of the race fighting a rearguard action. Half the battle of getting a clean start and hitting the line at speed is always knowing where the line is. Before the start, take a transit from one end of the line to an object on the shore, to which you can refer if one buoy is concealed by boards.

The first beat

Your course up the first beat will depend very much on your start. If you were slow off the line, it is pointless to sail in the 'dirty wind' of other boards, so you must tack off and head for free space where you can at least generate some board speed and perhaps pick up some favourable wind shifts.

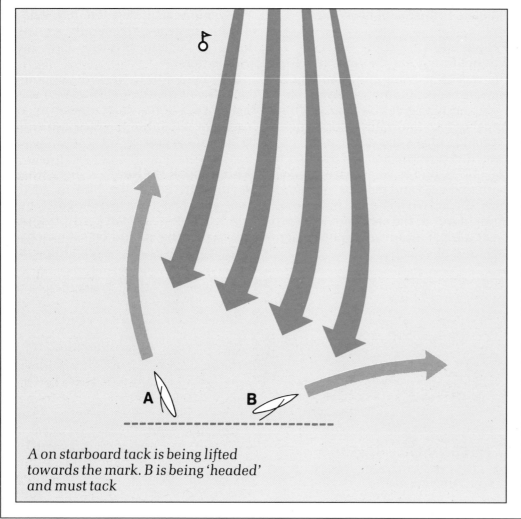

A on starboard tack is being lifted towards the mark. B is being 'headed' and must tack

The all-important start of a World Cup course race. Naish (USIIII) tries to pump into the lead. Should he find himself blanketed, he would have to tack off into 'clean air' to maintain his speed before attempting to make best use of the wind shifts and the currents

Wind shifts

The wind swings constantly about its mean direction. The extent of those shifts depends on the stability of the weather system and the shape of the surrounding land. Shifts arrive in the form of lifts and headers. The former 'lift' you up closer to the mark, while the latter force you further away. With experience you can feel the changes through your hands. If suddenly there is extra pressure in your front hand (as if you were bearing away), you are being lifted and can head up. If, on the other hand, the sail empties and you have to sheet in and bear away to maintain speed, you are being headed.

To tack or not to tack?

Whether you decide to tack to make use of a shift will depend on the wind strength and whether you think the wind will maintain its new direction or swing straight back. It can take up to seven seconds to complete a tack and accelerate back up to full speed, which in planing conditions can mean the loss of five or six board lengths. Such is the reason why up the shorter beats of a funboard course, competitors try to make just two tacks and suffer any minor headers in favour of board speed.

Whether you head to the left or right side of the course, or steam straight up the middle, will depend on where the tide is flowing strongest, where the wind is strongest and whether the land is in any way causing the wind to bend. Racing on the sea, for example, in a sideshore wind on a hot summer's day, the sea-breeze effect (the warm air rising off the land being replaced by the cooler air from the sea) causes the wind to bend slightly onshore. If you head towards the beach, therefore, you will be lifted up to the mark.

At other times, there is more wind out to sea. If you are unsure, it often pays to sail up the middle, a position from where you can head left or right should one side of the course appear attractive. By sailing immediately to one of the corners, you limit your options and can end up stranded.

The reaches

The 'rhumb' line is the direct course and the shortest distance between the two marks but is rarely the best one to follow unless you have a lead. Whether you decide to sail above or below the rhumb line will depend on the position of the next mark, the strength of the wind and the actions of the boards in front and behind you.

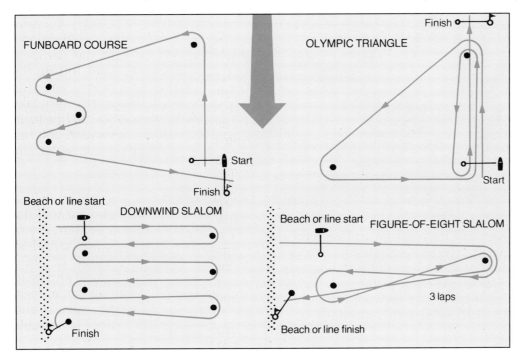

Course racing

1 When the fleet is large and of a good standard, as in this UK National Mistral Regatta, starting alone on port tack is a risky and often disastrous manoeuvre. Such was the case in this sequence, where ex-national champion Graeme Fuller makes a rare tactical error.

2 He spots that the start line is biased to port and, had he been quicker off the line, he might have crossed the fleet to be in a commanding lead. But, with five seconds to go he is stationary in the foreground, while the rest of the fleet, with right of way, are bearing down the line at full speed.

3 At the gun they are already on top of him and will be greeting him with cries of 'starboard', forcing him to take evasive action and tack in what little space is left for him.

4 The position is made even worse by the proximity of the windward boards, and he drops his sail. When he does eventually recover himself, most of the fleet will be to windward, forcing him to tack again simply to escape their dirty wind.

5 Thereafter he can only hope that fate has driven him to the favoured side of the beat and that he gets lifted to the mark ahead of his oppressors. If you do go for a port tack start, you must be totally committed and hit a gap in the line at full speed.

Having rounded the windward mark, the most natural course of action is to head high in order to overtake the leading boards to windward and take their wind. Moreover, by staying high, you will be the first to benefit from any gusts. As the gust arrives, you can bear away to stay with it and make up a lot of ground on the leeward boards. However, as a defensive measure, the leeward boards can 'luff' you – that is to say, sail well above their true course in order to squeeze you out upwind. If you arrive at the windward mark to see a number of boards engaged in a luffing battle, sailing a more direct low course, keeping out of their wind shadow, might well pay dividends.

To maintain speed on the reaches, you must use the waves. Always look ahead to see how they are forming

In order to move the track forwards (left), depress the release pedal, angle the mast back and lean down on the booms. Initially, you will find

it easier to sheet out. In order to move it back (right), depress the pedal, stay sheeted in and lift up on the booms

and pick a line through them. Always pump as you go down the face to generate enough speed to make it over the back of the next one. Pumping on top of the wave merely forces the tail deeper into the water. If you start to

come off the plane, harden up to the wind and then bear away again, preferably down the face of a wave, as the board picks up speed, so that you are looping down towards the mark.

Mark rounding

A further advantage of sailing a low course towards the gybe mark is that you can hug the inside slot. Once you have established an overlap on the inside as you approach the buoy, you can shout 'water', at which command the windward board must move out and give you room to gybe. Many places can be won and lost at the marks. Your ability to gybe in tight spaces inside the scrum may often reward you handsomely; inability to judge the size of gaps, on the other hand, can produce untold carnage, as board after board ploughs into the back of you. Often the best policy is to tuck in behind the board ahead and save your challenge for the reach. Always give yourself room to gybe inside him should he leave a gap or to take evasive action should he fall.

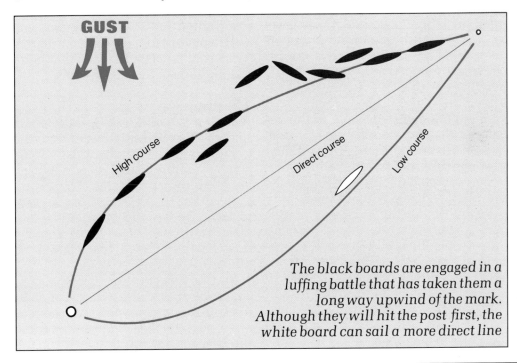

GUST

High course

Direct course

Low course

The black boards are engaged in a luffing battle that has taken them a long way upwind of the mark. Although they will hit the post first, the white board can sail a more direct line

Slalom

In slalom, the right of way rules favour the leading board. Here green is legally barged out downwind by pink as he tries to overtake at the finish

Of all the racing disciplines, slalom is undoubtedly the most exciting. As well as being easy to set up, the action is fast and furious, takes place close to shore and is easy to follow. From the windsurfer's point of view it is the ultimate test of short board gybing and board speed, and, far from being a suitable option for the tactically inept, split-second timing and judgment are required if you are to break away from the pack and hold the lead.

The courses
Slalom is run over either a figure-of-eight 'ins and outs' course or a five-mark downwind course. The latter is favoured in large competitions since one heat can be started while the other is still in progress, thereby speeding up the programme. The competition is run in heats containing, for safety reasons, no more than eight boards, on either a straight knock-out basis with the top four going through to the next round, or a double elimination system where losers go into a separate bracket for a second chance.

The rules
Due to the speed of the action and the difficulty of deciding protests, rules in slalom have been made gloriously simple. There is one fundamental understanding: the overtaking board keeps clear. This is a rule that applies equally on the reaches and around the marks. Until an overtaking board is clear ahead of your bow, you are allowed to sail above or below your true course to impede his progress. Overtaking, therefore, is difficult when the sailors are of similar standard. Most challenges happen during the gybes with often chaotic results – heated confrontations are frequent.

Slalom techniques
Acceleration and board speed are the slalom sailor's chief weapons, the former ultimately being more potent than the latter. In general, the legs are quite short and, due to the problems of overtaking on the reaches, places are usually gained either at the start or coming out of gybes, when acceleration is the key.

The fin plays a vital role in this respect. Slalom boards need some volume to support a big rig and float through lulls, but it is the sailor's aim, when powered up, to be sailing on the fin alone. This is a feat that is only possible if the fin is large and stiff enough to convert the lateral pressure of a camber induced sail into lift without spinning out. Having confidence in the fin allows the sailor to sheet in against the back foot to obtain instant lift and acceleration without the need to come out of the straps to coax the board on to the plane.

The jumps
Slalom in breaking waves is not unlike a steeple chase. No sooner have you settled into your stance than you have to negotiate a wall of water and somehow maintain your speed and your form. Over chop you can keep the board in contact with the water by bending and retracting the knees. Confronted by waves, however, you will unavoidably become airborne. Your goal must be to make that jump as long and shallow as possible.

The pre-jump
Just as a downhill skier will retract his legs just before a bump to avoid being launched upwards, some sailors pre-jump small waves using a chop hopping technique. The advantage is that they take off in the clear water in front of the wave and land in clear water the other side, thereby missing the aerated foam which so often provokes spin-out.

In the bigger surf, the size and shape of the wave will affect your plan. If the wave is big and steep, it often pays to sheet out as you climb the face so that you flop over the top

When the waves are this big, huge jumps in the slalom are unavoidable (top). To hold off challengers, Montague approaches the mark high so that he can maintain his windward position (middle left). Van den Berg on his way to victory sails in between the waves (middle right). In fifty knots of wind survival is the only tactic (bottom)

without wasting time in the air and risking a momentous fall.

Sailing over white water requires good timing and light-footedness. As it approaches, you must weight the back foot quickly to lift the nose, and then immediately lift the heels to allow the water to wash under the tail. If you leave your weight on the back foot, you could spin out or be washed backwards.

A fall in the waves will almost certainly mean a swim back to shore and exit from the competition, so, in very big waves, knowing your limitations can often save the day. During a dramatic World Cup slalom in La Torche, France, Hawaiian Peter Cabrinha, in the lead, was faced by an enormous pitching wave which threatened to swallow him whole. Rather than try to blast through it, he gybed in front of it and rode it back to the beach before turning round and heading back out to the mark for a second try. The rest of the fleet had meanwhile been swept away, having displayed less caution, and Cabrinha went through to the next round.

The slalom gybe

To gain places or defend a lead, your gybing in slalom must be tight and fast. Unlike gybing a short board for fun, in slalom you are probably holding a large sail and are just slightly overpowered, the water will be choppy and you may well have to cope with the spray, wash and dirty wind of the boards in front of you. Moreover, depending on your position and the position of the buoy, you may have to alter the radius of the turn at a moment's notice.

Slalom

The biggest problem with gybing big sails is how to control the power. A technique has been developed to turn that power to good effect. When you initiate the turn, lean the rig right in to leeward and oversheet it. This reduces the effective area while the rig drives in the turning edge and keeps the board level nose to tail. The body leans right forwards on to the mastfoot. The back hand holds in the sail until the very last minute and then throws the boom away for a fast rig change.

Much trial and error is needed to ascertain to what extent you can bury the inside rail without tripping up. The advantage is that with the board more level, the tail does not exert a braking effect. Instead, the energy is stored in that edge and, as the board is flattened out, you are projected at full speed on to the next reach, despite the tightness of the arc.

The start
For the benefit of the spectators, slaloms, wherever possible, used to start from the beach with sailors, in 'Le Mans' style, running with their boards into the water. Although this method is still used when conditions are too rough to launch a committee boat, it is generally considered unfair. The windward board has a huge advantage, and the shorebreak can dump on some sailors while offering others a few feet away a clear passage to launch.

Most competitions now feature a line start, which is both fairer and more skilful. The line is set roughly across the wind, although a good race officer will stagger it slightly, with the leeward end further forwards so that everyone can start on the line in clear wind. Although good course racers tend to fare well at line starts, the slalom technique is quite different. The slalom board's lack of volume means that you cannot stand on the line and sheet in when the gun goes; it is imperative to hit the line at full speed. The skill lies, therefore, in knowing how long it will take you to cover a certain distance.

Tom Luedecke demonstrates the slalom gybe, sheeting in hard, keeping the board flat and driving the whole length of the leeward rail into the water for a fast, tight turn

With a minute to go, you should be facing towards the line either moving slowly or in the waterstart position. With about twenty seconds remaining you should rise up, sheet in and begin to accelerate so that you hit a gap in the line in clean air as the gun goes. As in course racing, the line may well have a favoured end, but it is so short that any advantage will be quite small. Your priority is always to get away cleanly.

1 Speed through the waves relies on you ironing out the terrain with a soft knee action and keeping jumps long and flat. As you climb the face . . .

2 . . .lift the knees violently, drawing the tail up under your bottom. Stay sheeted in and maintain mastfoot pressure to keep a shallow trajectory.

3 Note how the board is being sailed through the air with the slot closed so that the sailor can land at speed, on the plane.

Wave contests

Naish delivers a crippling mental blow to Bruce Wylie in the early stages of a wave heat (left). When the waves are gutless or spasmodic, you can impress the judges and pile on the points with skills such as the body drag (below)

Wave contests are undeniably spectacular. Their obvious drawback is that, with the exception of a few exotic locations, the right conditions rarely arrive on the appointed day or last long enough for the completion of all the rounds.

Like slalom, wave contests are run on a single or double elimination basis. Depending on the numbers taking part, the heats consist of two or four players, and last between five and twenty minutes.

The judging

A constant criticism of wave contests in general is the subjective nature of the judging and scoring system. Traditionally, equal marks are awarded for jumps, wave riding and transitions (tacks and gybes), with bonus points for style, fluidity and originality. As a competitor, you must try to find out as much about the scoring system, and the judges themselves, as possible. Do they award marks for semi-completed manoeuvres? Are they looking for a clean, polished routine or do they want to see people going for outrageous tricks regardless of the consequences? Will all your manoeuvres count or will you be scored on just your best four waves? Do the judges themselves have any favourite manoeuvres?

Equipment

Contests are usually run in a minimum wind strength of fifteen knots, although it is quite feasible that the wind will drop below that during your heat. The old excuse, "There wasn't enough wind for my board," however valid, sounds pathetically weak, so you must be prepared, preferably with at least two boards and rigs ready on the beach. In the European rounds of the World Cup, where the wave conditions are usually less than perfect, the stars often take out their floaty high-wind slalom boards in preference to their wave boards. When the waves are mushy and slow, they need to generate speed for big jumps and to lend their wave riding manoeuvres some 'zip'. Their small wave boards are often too slow.

The contest

You are given a minute to launch and get out on the water before your heat starts. Use the time well so that you either launch into a jump or catch a wave as the gun goes. Robby Naish, for example, likes to deliver a crippling psychological blow to his opponent by performing a radical manoeuvre right in front of him in the first few seconds.

Success in the waves is centred around confidence. Many brilliant performers fail in contests because they hurry everything, become tense and try more difficult tricks to get themselves out of trouble. A far better plan is to start off simply with a trick you know you can do well to set you in the right frame of mind. For instance, heading out a short way and then gybing on a small wave right in front of the judges will ensure that they see you and that you are off the mark.

Most judges are impressed by variety. Start with an easy carve gybe inshore, for example, then next time do a duck gybe, then a one-handed carve. Show your versatility by throwing in a tack, all the time abiding by the golden rule: stay in the contest area.

You might perform the first triple loop ever, but if you did it half a mile down the beach out of sight of the rostrum, then you would score no points. It sounds simple, but with the more spectacular skills all being downwind manoeuvres, it is very easy to drift away unawares.

Speed sailing

Just twelve years ago speed sailing was the domain of a hardy band of eccentrics whose weird and wonderful craft punctuated the shores of Portland harbour once a year at the Weymouth speed trials. A few windsurfers were admitted under sufferance but were never considered a threat, especially not in the light of the catamaran Crossbow's incredible world speed sailing record of over thirty six knots.

Since that time, windsurfers have come to dominate speed trials around the world and in 1986 one piloted by Pascal Maka broke Crossbow's record by more than two knots to become the world's fastest sailing craft. It is a highly professional branch of windsurfing and one that has started to challenge the World Cup in terms of media coverage. For the manufacturers it is the perfect testing ground for new designs. Fully-battened sails, RAFs and camber inducers were all conceived as a result of information gained from speed trials.

Its enormous popularity stems from the fact that you are in competition with yourself and the clock, not your fellow competitor. Moreover, everyone likes going fast and, although the world's best are very skilful sailors, you do not have to be a brilliant windsurfer to experience the exhilaration of sailing a windsurfer down a speed course and recording a very respectable time.

The course
The standard speed sailing course is 500 metres long. The time the sailor takes to pass between the two transits is recorded and then the average speed is calculated. Such a course demands a sizeable stretch of water, however, and organizers are experimenting with 100-metre courses. The times, although not accepted for official world rankings, are expected to be higher since there is more chance of the wind remaining constant over the shorter distance.

The conditions
Potential world record breakers demand gale-force winds (in excess of thirty five knots), blowing at 120 degrees over completely flat water. At the best speed courses in the world, such as Weymouth in the UK, Port St Louis in southern France and Sotavento in the Canaries, the prevailing wind blows offshore across shallow water, resulting in only a very small build-up of chop.

The equipment
So specialized is the sport that the best have a quiver of boards and sails for every conceivable wind strength and water condition. Trim is so delicate that if they need to change down sail, they will change down board as well. They have different designs for different speed courses. Boards to be used on the choppy waters of Brest harbour will have more rocker than those designed for the smooth track at Sotavento.

The boards, more like water-skis, are very low volume, extremely narrow (less than 13 inches) for straight-line control, with small wetted areas for minimum drag. The underwater

Once the home of eccentrics and their magnificent sailing machines, speed trials are now dominated by windsurfers. Professionalism now prevails as the best fight it out for five-figure prize money

Tandems were mocked until the French pair, Griessman and Bertin, clocked 36 knots in the Canaries. Many now believe they are potentially faster than single boards. Here, Peter Hart and Dee Caldwell steer their 'Carlsberg Blue' to second place in the A class at the 1984 Weymouth trials

shape and the rocker line are critical. The design is ultimately a compromise since what might be the fastest shape in theory may be impossible to keep on the water. Most boards have sharp pintails – perhaps not the fastest contour shape, but one that gives a clean water release and holds the tail in contact with the water.

The sails are now seen as the area where the greatest advances will be made. The winner, now that sailing standard is so high, will be the one whose sail works most efficiently under the greatest strain. In fifty knots of wind, it must hold its shape, twist just the right amount always to display a clean profile to the wind and generate controllable power. Some sailors continue to experiment with solid foils but with limited success. If conditions are perfect, they might hold the answer, but they work badly if the wind is unstable.

Looking down the barrel of one of Fred Haywood's speed guns, less than thirteen inches wide

Technique

There was a time when the sailor who could hang on to the largest sail in a given wind won. Bulk was all-important. Fred Haywood fattened himself up on ice-cream before the Weymouth trials of 1984, but subsequently decided that a good strength to weight ratio was better than blubber. Today's speed sailor is very fit and strong with superb reactions. Now that excellent times are being recorded by both the large and the small sailor, it is obvious that technique is the deciding factor.

The sitting stance a speed sailor adopts is no different from that of a course racer or a slalom sailor, but with places being decided by hundredths of a second, that stance, together with the trim of the board and sail, has to be perfect. Like a skier holding his aerodynamic 'tuck', the speed sailor has to settle into his best rigid sailing position and, from the time he crosses the first transit to the time he finishes, must not disrupt the sail an inch. If he sheets out for a second, his time will suffer.

The timers can only register sailors at about ten-second intervals. As a result, many times are not recorded if the sailors arrive in a bunch. To avoid having your record-shattering time missed, time your run and keep an eye on the movements of the other sailors. The tiny boards often take a while to waterstart, so it is wise to start the run a long way back so that you have been travelling at full tilt for some time before you hit the line. Anyone who attempts to start in front of you should receive a loud verbal warning of your arrival.

The inconsistencies in the wind make it essential to fit in as many runs as possible in the hope of finding that lucky gust. Those who can gybe their boards and sail them back without the help of a support boat often reap the rewards.

A change in the format is anticipated where the week will be run like a regatta. Every day will count as a separate race, with the winner being the one who has accumulated the best times in a variety of conditions. Nevertheless, the majority will still have that treasured world speed record in their sights!

Glossary

Aerial
The prefix signifying that a manoeuvre is completed clear of the water, e.g. 'aerial gybe', 'aerial off-the-lip' etc.

Apparent wind
The wind felt by the windsurfer, being the combination of the true wind and his headwind.

Asymmetric board
A board designed for consistent wave conditions, with both sides of the board displaying contrasting turning characteristics.

Bail out
To desert in midair, when landing from an aerial manoeuvre threatens to be impossible or uncomfortable.

Bear away
To alter course away from the wind.

Beating upwind
Sailing a zigzag course to reach a windward destination.

Camber
The forward fullness in a sail.

Carve
To turn the board when on the plane by depressing the inside edge.

Custom boards
Non-production, hand-made boards, shaped, sprayed and laminated by hand to suit the exact needs of the individual.

Ding
Impact damage where the skin of the board is ruptured. Dings need instant repair.

Dump
Waves 'dump' when they peak and break in the same movement. This wave action is common on steeply shelving beaches.

Foil
The shape of an aircraft's wing. It is reproduced on sails, fins and daggerboards, and its smoothness greatly influences speed, lift and performance.

Funboard
A board of any length that is designed to perform in strong winds. Essential features include a fully-retractable centreboard and footstraps.

Gun
A long, narrow board designed for speed and control in strong winds which borrowed its shape from big-wave surfboards.

Gybe
A downwind turn where the back of the board passes through the eye of the wind.

Head up
To head up, or 'luff up', means to alter course towards the wind.

Knot
A measurement of speed, equal to one nautical mile per hour. One nautical mile (2,000 yards) denotes one minute of latitude.

Laminar flow
Smooth, uninterrupted airflow over the sail.

Leeward
Downwind. The leeward side is the side of the board furthest away from the wind.

Lip
The crest of a wave the moment before it breaks. The lip is the fastest, most critical section of the wave.

Luff
The leading edge of the sail. 'Luffing the sail' means to sheet out to spill wind, causing the sail to flap, or 'luff'.

Marginal board
A board with enough volume to float at rest but which starts to sink as you uphaul the rig.

Marginal wind
Wind that is barely strong enough to allow for planing.

Mastfoot
The connection between the rig and the board.

Mastfoot pressure
The application of force through the rig into the board via the mastfoot.

Mylar/Melinex
A light, stable polyester film used for sails.

Nose
The front section of the board.

One design
A racing class of identical boards, considered to be the fairest form of competition. Mistral and Windsurfer are the most active in this area.

Peel
Waves 'peel' when they break smoothly from one end to the other.

Plane
To sail on top of, rather than through, the water at high speed.

Port
The port side is the left side when facing the direction of travel, and is indicated by the colour red.

Production boards
Boards made in a mould using a uniform manufacturing process. For a board to qualify for the Production World Championships, a minimum series of 500 must be made.

Pump
To move the sail to increase the airflow over it and so promote earlier planing or more speed. It is illegal in some regattas, but encouraged in others.

Radical
An outmoded, over-used piece of surfing vernacular describing moments of extreme bravery/skill/foolhardiness on the water.

Rail
The edge of the board. 'Railing upwind' means heeling the board to windward so that the leeward rail engages in the water and increases the sideways grip.

Rocker
The scoop of the board as viewed from the side, e.g. nose rocker and tail rocker.

Sheeting in or out
Altering the sail's angle to the wind.

Slot flusher
Also known as the 'slot gasket' or 'flushing strip', the slot flusher comprises two strips of rubber or mylar which cover the centreboard slot to present a smooth surface to the water. It is famous for ripping off in the middle of a race.

Spin-out
The result of the fin suddenly losing its grip on the water due to air being sucked down both sides to form a complete pocket.

Starboard
The starboard side is the right side when facing the direction of travel, and is indicated by the colour green.

Tack
A change of direction where the front of the board passes through the eye of the wind.

Tail
The rear section of the board.

Tinkler Tail
Named after its inventor, the Tinkler Tail is a spring-loaded tail with a variable rocker line.

Trim
The act of balancing either the sail or the board. Trimming the sail involves sheeting in or out to find the sail's most efficient angle relative to the wind. Trimming the board means adjusting its position through foot and mastfoot pressure so that it lies at its most efficient angle in the water.

UJ
Universal joint, otherwise known as the 'power point'. It is the joint, usually made of rubber, at the base of the mast which allows the rig to fall in any direction.

Waterline length
The term denoting the length of the wetted area. A long waterline length often improves upwind performance.

Wetted area
The part of the board in contact with the water at any one time.

Windward
Upwind. The windward side is the side of the board nearest to the wind.

Wipe-out
A spectacular, involuntary dismount.

Index

Numerals in *italics* refer to illustrations

Index

Sinker(s), 24
Skeg, *see* Fin(s)
  box, 28, 48
Skiing, 12, *78*, 100, 108, 150, 155
Slalom, 13, 114, 119, 140, *147*, 150–52, *150*, *151*, *152*
  boards, *24*
  gybe, 151–52, *152*
  start, *140*, 152
Slam gybe, 64, 114–15, *114–15*
Sleight, Mike, 125
Slot, closing the, *82*, 142
Slot flusher, 141, 157
Soft sail, 35, *35*
Speed gun, *155*
Speed sailing, 33, 154–55, *154*, *155*
Speed-sailor, 15, 117
Spin-out, 27, 103, 130, 139, 141, 150, 157
Spin tack, *see* Helicopter tack
Spreader bar, 40–41
Stance, 53, 79, 82, 85–86, 94, 95, 102
  basic, 59, *59*
  beating, *144*
  funboard, 80–81, *81*
  poor, *69*, *80*, 89, 100
Stanley, Larry, 11
Starboard, 157
Static balance, 79
Steamer, 37, *38*
  dry, 37
Steering, 61
  on a run, 63, *63*, 64
  principles of, 19, *19*
  towards the wind, *61*
'Storm dagger', 11
Surf Line 'Egg', 12
Surfing, *78*, 137
Swell, *126*, 128, 137

T

Table top jump, *132*, 133, 136
Tack(s), 64, 66–67, *66–67*, 147, 157
  carve, 120, *120*
  duck, 124, *124–25*
  fast, 78
  helicopter, 121, *121*
  jump, 67
  short board, 119–21, *119*, *120*, *121*
Tacking, 16, *17*
Tail, *20*, 21, 157
  asymmetric, 21, *21*
  sink, 123
Ten Cate, 12
Thrusters, 27, *27*
Tides, 73
Timing, 79, 88, 95, 113, 129, 139
  poor, 113, *113*
'Tinkler Tail', 21–22, 157
Top turn(s), 138–39, *138*
Triangle racing, 12, *147*
Trim, 16, 78, 102, 154, 157
  angle, of sail, 18, 102
  board, 53, 137
Trimming
  the board, 81, 132, 137
  the sail, 132
True wind, 16, *16*
Tuition, 71
Turns
  bottom, 110, 137–38, *137*, *138*
  carved, 78
  top, 138–39, *138*

U

Universal joint (UJ), *33*, 49, 157
Uphauling, 56–57, *56*, 87, 92
Upwind recovery, 56, 57, *57*

V

Visualization, 51, 70
Volume, 20–21, 108

W

Waist harness, 40, *40*
  with nappy attachment, 40, *40*
Walze, Mike, 10
Waterstart, 87, 92–96, *94*, *95*,
  clew first, 106, *106*, 116, 117
  errors in, 95, *96*
  light-wind, 104–105, *104*, *105*
  practice for, 95–96, *96*
Wave boards, 24
Wave performance, 13, 140, 153, *153*
Weather
  conditions, 117
  forecasting, 72
Weight distribution, 117, 137
Wetsuit(s), 37, *37*, *39*, 74, 123
Wetted area, 21, *82*, 157
Weymouth speed trials, 154
  1984, 155, *155*
Whyte, Richard, 111
'Wimp stick', 45
Wind, 103
  apparent, 16, *16*, 113, 156
  direction, 126–27, *126*, *127*, 139
  head-, 16, *16*
  offshore, 72
  shifts, 147
  strong, 110
  true, 16, *16*
  using the, 57
'Wind Weapon', *136*
Windblown waves, 127, 137
Windglider, 12, 14, 24
Windsurfer, 10, 11, 12, 122
  One Design Class, 10, 140
  Rocket, 11, 12
  sail, 32
Windward, 157
'Wing', 33, *34*
Winner, Ken, 10, *73*
Wipe-out, 49, 157
World Cup, 13, 14
Wylie, Bruce, *153*

Acknowledgements

The author would like to thank the following:

Club Mistral, Barbados, and especially Phil, Randal and Rea without whose boat nothing would have been possible.

Paul Rapson and Ingrid at the Barbados Windsurfing Club for their unfailing hospitality.

The Caribbean Alternative.

Simon Bassett and Richard at Dee Caldwell's Sailboard Centre, West Wittering.

Mark Bennett and Barry Millington of Chichester Windsurfing.

Cliff Webb for his professional brilliance and for not shooting all my mistakes; and for supplying all the photographs in the book.

Michelle Pearce for her patience both on and off the water.